THE SNAKE THAT ROARS

"Be sober, be vigilant; because your adversary the devil, as a roaring lion, walketh about, seeking whom he may devour." – 1 Peter 5:8

Linda Eddy

Published by: **Kidron Valley Publishing and Promotions**
www.kidronvalleypublishing.com

THE SNAKE THAT ROARS
Copyright © 2013 by Linda Eddy

© All rights reserved.

Published in the U.S.A.

ISBN 978-0-9883915-0-5

All Scripture verses are quoted from the *Authorized King James Version* (KJV) unless otherwise noted.

Scripture quotations marked (NIV) are taken from the Holy Bible, New International Version®, NIV®. Copyright © 1973, 1978, 1984, 2011 by Biblica, Inc.™ Used by permission of Zondervan. All rights reserved worldwide. www.zondervan.com The "NIV" and "New International Version" are trademarks registered in the United States Patent and Trademark Office by Biblica, Inc.™

Cover Design by Tony and Terri Charles, and Linda Eddy

Cover *"Crush"* Graphic Image by Oxygen. All Images provided by Oxygen, ©2012 Sermonview and/or its licensors. All rights reserved. Used by permission.

Dedication

This book is dedicated to my special friend, Terri, without whom I would not have begun my effort to write it.

I also wish to extend a special note of thanks to my pastor, Chuck Lawrence, for writing the forward to this book, and for being a caring and supportive pastor.

~ Linda Eddy

Acknowledgements

I want to acknowledge and recognize the people and avenues that God used in my life. "It is written," Romans 13:7 states, "Render therefore to all their dues; tribute to whom tribute is due, custom to whom custom; fear to whom fear; honor to honor."

I wish to acknowledge those in the Body of Christ who were obedient to bring me books to read, CD's to listen to, and DVD's to watch. Also, I wish to acknowledge those men and women who, by the spirit of God, have written books that God used to feed my spirit—everyone from Oliver B. Green, to Kenneth Hagin, Kenneth Copeland, Smith Wigglesworth, Madame Guyon, Watchmen Nee, and everyone in-between.

Also, I wish to acknowledge those faithful shepherds that God chose and anointed to teach me His principles and His word: my pastor of many years, Darrell Huffman; my current pastor, Chuck Lawrence, who is faithful and mighty in the Scriptures; and, Pastor Joe Snipes who is also mightily anointed and ministered life unto me.

Last, but not least, I wish to acknowledge *Rhema Bible School,* which was life-changing for me. The Bible came alive and personal to me. The hand of God was certainly upon that place and flowed out to the students. *Life Christian University,* based in Florida, also filled me with a love and life of the Scriptures.

The Bible represents the whole counsel of God. Seek it with a humble heart; you will be filled with righteousness and the purposes of God. I want to also thank my granddaughter, Mariah, and my daughter Jodi, without their help this book could not have been completed. I want to also acknowledge my son

Josiah, of whom his birth was announced by the word of the Lord; his life also being a testimony of the word of God.

– Linda Eddy

Table of Contents

Foreword 9
Part A - "At the Beginning" 11
Part B - "Being Established" 41
Part C - "Consistently Maintaining 77

Foreword

No matter how many times we hear it, we are frequently in need of the reminders that Linda Eddy brings to us in the pages of this book. *Satan is a counterfeit* and *a deceiver;* his only power over us is the power we allow him to have—if he is to gain any hold over us at all.

As Paul advised Timothy, **"...I know who I have believed and am convinced that he is able to guard what I have entrusted to him until that day,"** II Timothy 1:12b NIV.

This book provides us with a rich and varied list of reminders and admonishments from Scripture. In addition, Linda provides insights and encouragement for the believer. Linda draws on a rich experiential life of living out these reminders. Her life is an example of the Scriptures she draws on to walk out a life of treading on serpents and defeating the devil!

I encourage you to read this book and put these scriptural reminders in practice in your own life, and focus on the Lord—not on the devil and his counterfeit traps. God is greater, and this reminder can help you to see that and to not be caught up in the flypaper of Satan's deceit.

Chuck Lawrence
Senior Pastor
Christ Temple Church, Huntington, WV

— Part A —

At The Beginning

Throughout the Bible, "the snake," the old serpent, is referred to as the devil, Satan, and the Evil One.

Revelation 12:9 KJV
And the great dragon was cast out, that old <u>serpent, called the Devil, and Satan</u>, which deceiveth the whole world: he was cast out into the earth, and his angels were cast out with him.

He confuses and deceives the minds and hearts of God's people, claiming that he is like a powerful lion; but, in truth, he is a snake under their feet!

Where did the snake come from? The Bible tells us God created the serpent [snake] that eventually deceived Eve in the garden.

Genesis 3:1 NIV
Now <u>the serpent</u> was more crafty than any of the wild animals <u>the Lord God had made</u>. He said to the woman, Did God really say, 'You must not eat from any tree in the garden'? [Emphasis added]

The Scripture states that the snake was created by God. The snake had no creative power of his own. He was in submission to the God of all creation. His lies and deceitfulness brought him under a curse, and he was condemned for an eternity as a defeated foe. In God's eyes, Satan has no power or authority over God's beloved family, of which you and me are a part [the church].

In Scripture, when you discover a person, place, thing, or principle, its initial meaning is consistently the same throughout the Bible, only the intensity can be multiplied in the way it is used. So, let's look at the first time the word "serpent" is used in the Bible:

Genesis 3:1 NIV
Now the <u>serpent</u> was more <u>crafty</u> [sly, deceitful] than any of the wild animals the Lord God had made. He said to the woman, "Did God really say, 'You must not eat from any tree in the garden'"?

We can see that the Scriptures identify the serpent as being *deceitful.* He continues to be deceitful in the New Testament. We are warned that the devil (the serpent) will try to deceive us by appearing to be a vicious lion in order to scare us into thinking we cannot fight against him, thus, allowing him to devour us!

1 Peter 5:8 KJV
Be sober, be vigilant; because your adversary the devil, [appears] <u>as a roaring lion</u>, walketh about, seeking whom he may devour.

Satan is described as a roaring lion going about seeking whom he may devour. However, he is *not* a lion; he is a *pretender,* or counterfeit, to the *real* Lion—the Lion of the tribe of Judah (Jesus Christ). Satan cannot devour everyone, only those who allow him—those who have been deceived by circumstances or voices of the mind and spirit. One's "spirit" is commonly referred to as their "heart." Within the word "heart" is the word "ear" [h**ear**t]; our heart is our spiritual ear.

Proverbs 20:27 KJV
The spirit of man is the candle of the LORD, searching all the inward parts of the belly.

God desires truth in the inward parts, our innermost being. Our hearts are God's arena. All of God's truth is revealed and deposited within our hearts. We need not search outwardly to know God's will and ways. Only seek and search for the truth within your own heart.

Psalm 51:6 KJV
Behold, thou desirest truth in the inward parts [spirit/heart]: and in the hidden part [heart] thou shalt make me to know wisdom.

In Genesis 3, God declares that mankind would bruise the head of the serpent and that the snake would bruise our heel.

Genesis 3:14-15 KJV
And the LORD God said unto the serpent, Because thou hast done this, thou *art* cursed above all cattle, and above every beast of the field; upon thy belly shalt thou go, and dust shalt thou eat all the days of thy life: And I will put enmity between thee and the woman, and between thy seed and her seed; it shall bruise thy head, and thou shalt bruise his heel.

We have authority and power over the snake—Satan, as he is called. Bruising his head reveals that we have authority over him. (The "head," in scripture, always refers to authority.) On the other hand, Satan bruising our heel infers that he attacks our life's journey as we walk it out.

Luke 10:18-19 KJV

And he said unto them, I beheld Satan as lightning fall from heaven. Behold, <u>I give unto you power to tread on serpents</u> and scorpions, and <u>over all the power of the enemy</u>: and nothing shall by any means hurt you.

Our authority and power is through the shed blood of Jesus Christ and the covenant of Almighty God to his creation, his family, of which you and I belong. We have all of God's power and authority residing within us, which is more than enough to cancel and destroy all of the capabilities of "the snake that roars" (Satan).

Luke 9:1 KJV

Then he called his twelve disciples together, and gave them <u>power and authority over all devils</u>, and to cure diseases.

Through God's word and his name, God has provided us with all of the power and authority that we need to stop the enemy's attacks in our lives. However, if you don't know it, you can't use it!

The Scriptures also foretell our victory and describes in what manner we receive and maintain that victory over "the snake that roars."

God spoke His truth into the earth and it was manifested in the flesh [natural arena]. God is still speaking today. He speaks His word, which reveals His heart. We are to live victorious over any assault that would come from the enemy.

Our new life starts the day we surrender to Jesus Christ. From this day forward, we are no longer in the kingdom of darkness or subject to its ruling and reigning over us. Therefore, we have been transformed into new creations—into the image of God. Because of this, we are under God's authority, living in his arena of life.

2 Corinthians 5:17 KJV

Therefore if any man be in Christ, he is a new creature: old things are passed away; behold all things are become new.

That day our covenant, with its marvelous promises and benefits, begins. The entirety of God's kingdom is ours through the shed blood of Jesus. There is truly "power, power, wonder-working power" in the blood of Jesus! All we have to do is receive; it is totally free!

Hebrews 6:12 KJV

That ye be not slothful, but followers of them who through faith and patience inherit the promises.

We cannot be lazy when it comes to producing victory in our lives through the skilled use of the word of God. God intends for us to be victorious through faith and patience in this life's journey. To inherit our promises, we must submit our insecurities and failures to God's word. Our feelings and emotions cannot rule and reign above the word of God in our lives.

Hebrews 8:6 KJV
But now hath he obtained a more excellent ministry, by how much also he is the mediator of a better covenant, which was established upon better promises.

Our spiritual life—meaning our Christian walk—is only established by the promises in God's word. Christ, by His death on the cross, had destroyed the law of sin and death; therefore, the promises of the covenant have been transferred to us.

2 Peter 1:4-5 KJV
Whereby are <u>given unto us exceeding great and precious promises</u>: that by these ye might be partakers of the divine nature, having escaped the corruption that is in the world through lust. And beside this, giving all diligence, add to your faith virtue; and to virtue knowledge.

We must each discover what that inheritance entails and how we can make it a reality in our lives. God is no respecter of persons; His inheritance is for *all* of his children! His heart is grieved when any of His children are walking in bondage or darkness—which the truth of his inheritance would expose and expel.

Acts 20:32 KJV
And now, brethren, I commend you to God, and to the word of his grace, which is able to build you up, and

to give you an inheritance among all them which are sanctified.

Acquiring our inheritance can only be done as we continue to seek God's presence and word. When we take time to be in God's presence with His word, He reveals His plan and purpose for our life—as well as exposing the enemy's tactics.

Hebrews 4:12 KJV
For the word of God is quick, and powerful, and sharper than any two edged sword, piercing even to the dividing asunder of soul and spirit, and of the joints and marrow, and is a discerner of the thoughts and intents of the heart.

We begin this new life with the word of God. We must learn to daily feed our spirits with the word of God—as it is our spiritual food [remember, what you don't feed dies]. Whatever deceit or darkness the "snake that roars" would deliver to us, God's word will analyze, expose, and destroy.

We also must continue to submit all that we are in this life to the word of God. All of our life's experiences and circumstances, good or bad, must be submitted to God's thoughts and ways. As we submit ourselves to the word of God, we will be sanctified.

1 Thessalonians 5:23 KJV
And the very God of peace sanctify you wholly; and I pray God your whole spirit and soul and body be preserved blameless unto the coming of our Lord Jesus Christ.

God has provided, in His word, the avenues of sanctification and deliverance for our spirit, soul, and body. He does not want any part of our life in subjection to the enemy. The truth of His word shines the light and sets us free!

Simply put, we must, on a continual basis, seek God's word which will produce His righteousness in our lives. Through the door of righteousness [right standing] all of God's kingdom can be transferred to us.

Matthew 6:33 KJV
But seek ye first the kingdom of God, and his righteousness; and all these things shall be added unto you.

All we have to do is receive God's word, thoughts, and ways into our lives. It becomes such an integral part of our lives as it is engrafted into our very souls. (The "soul" is our mind, will, and emotions.) Meekness simply means that we say "yes" to the word of God, and "no" to our feelings and emotions.

James 1:21 KJV
...Receive with meekness the engrafted word, which is able to save your souls.

It is our reasonable service to submit our minds and bodies to the truths and precepts found in the word of God.

Romans 12:1 KJV
...Present your bodies a living sacrifice, holy, acceptable unto God, which is your reasonable service.

So, you see that God, our heavenly Father made a way for us, His children, to be free and give him glory and honor in our spirit, soul, and body. He did not leave any part of our lives to be influenced or controlled by "the snake that roars." God loves His creation, His family, of which you and I belong.

The word of God tells us who we are, where we are going, and how to get there. It literally dissects us from within and reveals aspects of our spirit, soul, and body. Although Satan attempts to deceive us through these areas, the word of God will reveal his deceit—*and destroy it!*

Hebrews 4:12 KJV
For the word of God *is* quick, and powerful, and sharper than any two-edged sword, piercing even to the <u>dividing asunder of soul and spirit</u>, and of the joints and marrow, and is <u>a discerner of the thoughts and intents</u> of the heart.

God has magnified his word above his name!

Psalm 138:2 KJV
I will worship toward thy holy temple, and praise thy name for thy loving kindness and for thy truth: for <u>thou hast magnified thy word above all thy name</u>.

God himself bows to and honors his word above all. The angels carry out God's word when it is spoken aloud.

Psalm 103:20 KJV
Bless the LORD, ye <u>his angels</u>, that excel in strength, that <u>do his commandments, hearkening unto the voice of his word</u>.

As we believe and speak God's word, even the mighty angels move and work on our behalf! If we do not believe and speak God's word, they stand with arms crossed, waiting.

The anointing that destroys the yokes—which include all bondages in our spirit, soul and body—is subject to the word of God. The Spirit, Himself, moves on our behalf as we speak God's word. He (the Spirit) is *the executor* of God's will—which is His word—in all aspects of our Christian life.

Isaiah 10:27 KJV

And it shall come to pass in that day, that his burden shall be taken away from off thy shoulder, and his yoke from off thy neck, and the <u>yoke shall be destroyed because of the anointing</u>.

Jesus Himself declares that our life is dependent on the word of God.

Matthew 4:4 KJV

But he answered and said, It is written, Man shall not live by bread alone, but by every word that proceedeth out of the mouth of God.

All that we do, think, or see should be monitored and based only on God's principles. We can speak to our obstacles and seeming failures. What should we say to our obstacles and failures? We should quote God's word to these things.

This simple principle must become a priority in our lives. We should not speak our emotions, feelings, and opinions, but, rather, we should speak what God says to us, and about us.

Jesus destroyed all Satan's attempts to defeat him with the statement "it is written."

Matthew 4:10 KJV

Then saith Jesus unto him, get thee hence, Satan: for IT IS WRITTEN, Thou shalt worship the Lord thy God, and him only shalt thou serve.

The word was quoted to Satan by Jesus. Satan has no defense against the word of God coming from a believer's mouth in faith. Satan attacked Jesus in his spirit, his soul, and his body—as he does you and me; however, Satan could not succeed because of the word of God being spoken by Jesus. Our victory is achieved and maintained the same way—by simply believing and speaking God's word. The Spirit of God (the Holy Ghost), as well as angels, are present to carry out our commands according to God's word.

2 Corinthians 4:13 KJV

We having the same spirit of faith, according as it is written, I believed, and therefore have I spoken; we also believe, and therefore speak.

Jesus did *not* defeat Satan simply because he was the son of God from heaven, but Jesus defeated Satan by being a man born in the earth, anointed with the Holy Ghost, and *speaking the word of God.* My brother and sister, so are we sons and daughters born in the earth, anointed by God to speak and declare his word as it is revealed in our spirits. It is the anointing that gets the job done. *All we must do is speak God's word about the matter!*

Authority in the earth was taken from God's people through deceit and the misquoting of the Scriptures in the Garden of Eden. However, Jesus gave us back our authority over Satan!

Luke 10:19 KJV
Behold, **I give unto you power to tread on serpents and scorpions**, and over all the power of the enemy: and nothing shall by any means hurt you.

Jesus is able to give us power because he has all power.

Matthew 28:18 KJV
And Jesus came and spoke unto them, saying, **All power is given unto me in heaven and in earth.**

Satan is called the Great Deceiver because he twists the word of God, deceiving God's children into thinking that tradition and religion are more powerful than the truth of God's word.

God has spoken from the beginning, declaring that there will be a war between the natural and the spiritual.

Genesis 3:15 KJV
And I will put enmity between thee and the woman, and between thy seed and her seed; it shall bruise thy head, and thou shalt bruise his heel.

Satan attacks our natural lives with natural circumstances, but God has already given us victory and authority over Satan through the word of God and the anointing of the Holy Ghost in our lives. Jesus transferred His authority and power to His servants.

Luke 9:1 KJV

Then he called his twelve disciples together, and <u>gave them power and authority over all devils, and to cure diseases</u>.

We are not only His sons and daughters—but his servants also. We have that same authority and power at our disposal as did the original disciples. In order to access that authority and power, we must trust and speak the word of God.

Mark 3:14-15 KJV

And he ordained twelve, that they should be with him, and that he might send them forth to preach, And to have power to heal sicknesses, and to cast out devils.

God has called and ordained each one of us for the glory of His kingdom. That same power to heal sicknesses and cast out devils is within *us*. We must know who we are in Christ and understand that the same resurrection power that raised Jesus from the dead is within us, and quickens our mortal body the same way!

Romans 8:11 KJV

But if the Spirit of him that raised up Jesus from the dead dwell in you, he that raised up Christ from the dead shall also quicken your mortal bodies by his Spirit that dwelleth in you.

Authority was given back to God's people through a man anointed of God, speaking the word of God. Who was this man? It was Jesus who is the *true* lion—the Lion of the tribe of Judah.

God had given total power and authority to his children—Adam and Eve, in the Garden of Eden.

Genesis 3:15 KJV
And I will put enmity between thee and the woman, and between thy seed and her seed; it shall bruise thy head, and THOU SHALT BRUISE HIS HEEL.

As we have already seen, there is a spiritual war going on. However, we are the victors! Spiritual power and laws always have ascendency over natural abilities. God knew and declared that this spiritual war between man and Satan would happen. In preparation, God ordained that all of His power and authority would be ours to use.

Genesis 1:26 KJV
And God said, Let us make man in our image, after our likeness: and let them (mankind) HAVE DOMINION OVER the fish of the sea, and over the fowl of the air, and over the cattle, and over all the earth, and over every creeping thing that creepeth upon the earth.

Mankind had power and authority over all creation under them, including all the animal kingdom, all the fowls, all the fish. They had total dominion over all—**INCLUDING THE SERPENT!** Unfortunately, however, in the weakness of their flesh and lust of their eyes, they listened to the snake as he spoke his lies and misquoting of the word of God.

Adam and Eve also did not interpret the word of God correctly. God had actually instructed them not to "eat" of the tree of knowledge of good and evil (Gen 2:17); however, Eve told the serpent that God had said they should not even "touch" it

(Gen. 3:3). Thus, by misquoting God's word, she revealed to Satan that she was unknowledgeable and unskillful in use of God's word.

The most important thing in our life is to recognize and receive the word of God *as it is written*. We must also learn to obey without question.

2 Timothy 2:15 KJV

<u>Study</u> to show thyself approved unto God, a workman that needeth not to be ashamed, <u>rightly dividing the word of truth</u>.

If we truly know and believe the word of God, we will not be deceived by Satan in any desire or circumstance. Satan wants to keep the word of God from producing faith in our lives. He knows that faith will stop any fiery dart that he may shoot at us.

Ephesians 6:16-17 KJV

Above all, taking the shield of faith, wherewith ye shall be able to quench all the fiery darts of the wicked. And take the helmet of salvation, and the sword of the Spirit, which is the word of God.

Faith is a simple thing. It is not hard to perceive. If you remember the acronym <u>F</u>ather <u>A</u>lways <u>I</u>n <u>T</u>he <u>H</u>eart [FAITH]. With the Father's presence in our hearts, faith is easy to understand. We are to live our daily lives by faith. God only moves according to our faith in him, which is established on our receiving and perceiving the word of God.

Romans 1:17 KJV
For therein is the righteousness of God revealed from faith to faith: as it is written, <u>the just shall live by faith</u>.

We have only one way to live—and that is *by faith*. Believing and submitting ourselves to the word of God produces His righteousness in our lives. As we walk our life by the faith of God, the righteousness of God will become a reality in our lives.

Our lives are only justified before our Father as we walk and live according to His word.

Galatians 3:11 KJV
But that no man is justified by the law in the sight of God, it is evident: for, the just shall live by faith.

God will not accept any excuses or justifications on our part other than submitting and obeying His word.

Hebrews 10:38 KJV
Now the just shall live by faith: but if any man draw back, my soul shall have no pleasure in him.

Here we see again: there is no way to please our Father except within the boundaries of His word. We must continue to check our lifestyle as to how it lines up with God's word. God's word does not change, so *we* must be the one to change. God's word is full of His great love and mercy. Submitting to the word is joyous to our hearts, but a little rough on our flesh.

So, we see, church, that the snake, the Old Serpent, does not want us to be aware of faith, the simplicity of knowing faith is just acknowledging the presence of <u>F</u>ather <u>A</u>lways <u>I</u>n <u>T</u>he <u>H</u>eart

[FAITH]. The fact of the matter is that we cannot please God if we do not live by faith!

Hebrews 11:6 KJV
But without faith it is impossible to please him: for he that cometh to God must believe that he is, and that he is a rewarder of them that diligently seek him.

So, we see in the beginning, God's word declares that the Old Serpent was created by God. We also see that Satan had no power or authority over mankind. In fact, just the opposite was true: Satan was *under* the dominion of God's man, Adam. But then, Satan used his subtle abilities to deceive and dethrone man's authority. God, Himself, declared that Satan's intended place in this life was to be *under* the foot of mankind. Through Jesus and our blood covenant, Satan is under our feet today!

Luke 10:19 KJV
Behold, I give unto you power to tread (walk) on serpents and scorpions, and over all the power of the enemy: and nothing shall by any means hurt you.

Brothers and sisters, Satan is a liar and a deceiver. He is *not* a lion. He is only *pretending* to be a lion with a loud roar, but he has no power to back it up.

Let us stand steadfast in faith declaring what God says. As we stand and declare the word of God, Satan cannot accomplish his evil pursuit.

There is only one way to be free from deceit and darkness, or any other thing that would keep us in bondage: and that is to have God's truth revealed to our hearts. Head knowledge does not free us, but heart knowledge does.

John 8:32 KJV
And ye shall know the truth, and the truth shall make you free.

We are sanctified, set apart from the world, healed, delivered and protected by the word of God.

John 17:17 KJV
Sanctify them through thy truth: thy word is truth.

All of our spiritual life must be done in and through the truth of God's statutes and ordinances. The snake cannot come in unless the hedge of God's word is down in our heart and mind.

We worship God only in the truth of the Scriptures, and we enter his presence with a heart full of love and devotion to Him.

John 4:24 KJV
God is a Spirit: and they that worship him must worship him in spirit and in truth.

True worship can only come from our hearts. God wants heart-to-heart worship and fellowship.

God is our example, he created us in his image, and that means we mimic his actions; in other words, do like he does. He spoke his word, and the Spirit moved to bring the spoken word into existence.

Genesis 1:3 KJV
And God <u>said</u>, Let there be light: and there was light.

Likewise, we speak the word as it is revealed to our hearts, and God's Spirit will bring it to pass. We do not have to worry about "how" this happens, as that aspect of it is *God's* arena—not ours. We need only worry about our part—which is believing God's word and then speaking it in faith.

The Spirit moves and begins the work of bringing the word of God into a reality in our own lives. It doesn't matter if we have a spiritual need, an emotional need, or physical need—the word of God has the answer, the solution. We must resist "the snake that roars," as well as conform to the instructions for us in God's word (to speak our faith aloud).

James 4:7 KJV
Submit yourselves therefore to God. Resist the devil, and he will flee from you.

Satan's greatest desire is to rob God of his glory. God's glory is only manifested in us as His truth is revealed and obeyed.

The devil is a liar, a deceiver, and a murder. He only counterfeits the truth as there is no real truth in him.

John 8:44 KJV
...[The devil] abode not in the truth, because there is no truth in him. When he speaketh a lie, he speaketh of his own: for he is a liar, and the father of it.

Every avenue of attack is for one reason: that reason being to destroy God's creation. Satan implies that he is of greater power; therefore, attempting to make a mockery of God and His kingdom.

We must cry out to God with a love for the truth that we be not deceived. The anointing and the truth of God's word will always expose darkness.

John 8:31-32 KJV
Then said Jesus to those Jews which believed on him, If ye continue in my word, then are ye my disciples indeed; And ye shall know the truth, and the truth shall make you free.

What is truth? Simply put, it is the written word of God and the spoken word of God which becomes a *rhema* word. The original New Testament writings were written in Greek and later translated into English. *Rhema* is a Greek word found in the original Scriptures which was translated as "word" in the English Bible. It is a specific type of "word." It specifically refers to a "revealed word" to our heart.

A revealed word is a word in the Scripture whose truth has been revealed to us by the Holy Spirit. This type of word "comes alive" in our hearts. It is a "knowing" within us. It is "heart knowledge," not "head knowledge." It is when a particular word of God is a reality in our lives.

Christ, Himself, is the Living Word.

John 1:14 KJV
<u>**And the word was made flesh**</u>**, and dwelt among us, [and we beheld his glory, the glory as of the only begotten of the Father,] full of grace and truth.**

Jesus is the Word, truly made flesh. He, Himself, reveals God. Jesus said, "If you've seen me, you've seen the Father" (John 14:9). Jesus revealed the Father's character, motives, thoughts, will, plan, and purpose for mankind. If you know who Jesus is, then you know the Father.

We must love the word of God more than our necessary food. We must realize that God's word truly is the bread from

Heaven. Everything we need in this life, whether spiritually, emotionally, or physically, is within the word of God. It will protect, provide, and nourish all aspects pertaining to these areas. Job said of God's word,

Job 23:12 KJV
...I have esteemed (valued) the words of his (God's) mouth more than my necessary food.

Brothers and sisters, the things of God—the spiritual kingdom—*must* be a priority in our lives. It has to be more important to us than fleshly, carnal appetites or lusts of our soul. If you will ask the Father, he will reveal to you how your fleshly thoughts and appetites are entering into your life.

1 John 2:16-17 KJV
For all that is in the world, the lust of the flesh, and the lust of the eyes, and the pride of life, is not of the Father, but is of the world. And the world passeth away, and the lust thereof: but he that doeth the will of God abideth for ever.

Every area of attack is through one of the gates: your spirit [heart], soul [your mind, will, and intellect], or the flesh [your body]. The definition of appetite is "a natural desire for satisfying a want or need."

We must have a heart that cries out to God for the love of the truth. If we love the truth, "the snake that roars" cannot keep us deceived. He has to bow to the spoken word of God being enforced by the Living Word, which is Christ, himself. Brothers and sisters, we must recognize and receive the truth of the Scriptures!

From the beginning Satan's sole purpose was to deny, destroy, and refute the word of Almighty God, who was his Creator. That same purpose is Satan's driving force today. God speaks words into our heart—*rhema* words, revealed words, words alive with the power and creative ability of Almighty God!

These words of God are seeds planted into our heart. These seeds must grow and mature, resulting in the word of God being manifested in our daily lives. However, after some people hear the word of God, Satan, "the snake that roars," comes immediately, and by deception, takes away the word that was sown in their hearts.

Mark 4:14-15 NIV

The farmer sows the word. Some people are like seed along the path, where the word is sown. As soon as they hear it, Satan comes and takes away the word that was sown in them.

God wants to create His Kingdom with all His glory and power in our lives. He wants to reveal himself through his body, which is the church—you and me. He does that by implanting the word on our spirit which matures and brings forth the fruit of righteousness, healing, deliverance, prosperity, protection—whatever God's people need, the word will produce freedom and liberty. That is why "the snake that roars" despises the word. The word will produce whatever we need, but we must hold fast to that which was planted.

We water the seed with regular praise, prayer, and confession. We must confess that the word is true. The word of God will not deceive. If we do not do these things to keep our seed alive, it will have no root within us. It is this root which keeps us connected to the Vine, which is Christ.

Mark 4:16-17 NIV
Others, like seed sown on rocky places, hear the word and at once receive it with joy. But since <u>they have no root, they last only a short time</u>. When trouble or persecution comes because of the word, <u>they quickly fall away</u>.

So, it is important that we take care of the root of the word that has been planted in us. If we neglect the root and we stop believing the word, "the snake that roars" has just deceived you and robbed you of God's word! Whatever God has spoken to your heart is what Satan desires to steal from you. It is not you or I that Satan cares about; his whole agenda is to cut off the word before it produces fruit in your life.

Mark 4:18-19 NIV
Still others, like seed sown among thorns, hear the word; but the worries of this life, the deceitfulness of wealth and the desires for other things come in and <u>choke the word, making it unfruitful</u>.

When we allow the cares of this world to overcome our minds, the word becomes unfruitful. The word will produce nothing if it has no roots. All it takes to keep the root alive and healthy is to water the word until harvest time. We water the seed of God's word by speaking it and thanking God for bringing it to pass—even before we see its fruition with our natural eyes.

We must have faith that God will bring his word to pass before it actually happens in the natural realm. So, we must claim God's promises, thanking and praising Him for bringing his word to pass in our lives—even before we see it happen. That is how we "water" the seed of God's word.

Water is the life of the seed; therefore, we must continually lift up our seed to God with a thankful and praising heart.

Job 14:7-9 NIV
At least there is hope for a tree: If it is cut down, it will sprout again, and its new shoots will not fail. Its roots may grow old in the ground and its stump die in the soil, yet at the scent of water it will bud and put forth shoots like a plant.

Praise the Lord, church! God has made a way for us to live in abundance! This is accomplished by his word being watered from the heavens. God himself sends forth His presence and anointing upon his word.

Ephesians 5:26 KJV
That he might sanctify and cleanse it (the church) with the washing of water by the word.

When "the snake that roars" comes with his lies and deceit, know that he is a defeated foe and he has to bow to the word of God. There is not any bondage, any fear, or any crippling circumstances that can alter or deter your destiny—if you will only believe and speak the word. The simplest, mightiest, and most marvelous truth in the Bible is that our lives, as we know them today and from now until eternity, depends on our knowing, believing and speaking God's word.

Matthew 4:4 KJV

But he answered and said, It is written, Man shall not live by bread alone, but <u>by every word</u> that proceedeth out of the mouth of God.

This important truth is so simple, yet so powerful that it can, and does, change every circumstance in our life. Our very existence, both naturally and spiritually, can and will be determined by the spoken word of God. God's spoken word will then manifest in the earth.

Church, we were created to rule and reign over all God's creation.

Genesis 1:26-27 KJV

And God said, Let us make man in our image, after our likeness: and let them have <u>dominion</u> over the fish of the sea, and over the fowl of the air, and over the cattle, and over all the earth, and over every creeping thing that creepeth upon the earth.

So God created man in his own <u>image</u>, in the image of God created he him; male and female created he them.

The term "image" means "mirror" or "reflect," also "a visual representation." Satan, by deceit and deception, has stolen our life of visual representation, but only temporarily. God gave back our ability to "mirror," to be "a visual representative" of God by the truth of his word.

We lost our inheritance, our authority, by not knowing God's word. We receive our lives with full assurance of our inheritances and all that is in God's kingdom by receiving and believing his word. Simple, simple, simple—that is why "the snake that roars" does everything that he can possibly do to keep us away from the simplicity of the truth in the Scriptures.

It is a mind game to get us to believe that what we see and feel is more real than the word of God. But this is a **lie**. Satan blinds people's minds from the glorious truths found in God's word.

2 Corinthians 4:3-4 KJV
But if our gospel be hid, it is hid to them that are lost: In whom the god of this world hath <u>blinded the minds</u> of them which believe not, lest the light of the glorious gospel of Christ, who is the image of God, should shine unto them.

But if our gospel be hid, it is hid to them that are lost. Lost means "veiled;" we cannot see. The "snake that roars" attacks our mind, our emotions, and our intellect to deceive, to lie, and to counterfeit the word of God so that we lose our inheritance, our covenant promises, and to ultimately rob God of his glory. He, the snake, cannot touch God so the next best thing is God's beloved creation—you and me.

We must reject any thoughts that Satan tries to put in our mind which are contrary to the word of God.

2 Corinthians 10:5-6 KJV
Casting down imaginations, and every high thing that exalteth itself against the knowledge of God, and bringing into captivity every thought to the obedience of Christ; and having in a readiness to revenge all disobedience, when your obedience is fulfilled.

Meaning, church, that quickly and steadfastly we reject any thought, any idea, or any emotion that is not submitted to the word of God. All aspects of our personality must bow to the word of God. We must be willing to submit all that we think and do to the scrutiny of God's word.

Isaiah 50:7 KJV
For the Lord God will help me; therefore shall I not be confounded: therefore have I set my face like a flint, and I know that I shall not be ashamed.

It is obedience, church—just simply doing what the word of God says. Trust God and obey Him. He and His word are one. The word will manifest God's glory, his power, and his authority in the earth. Even though my flesh and emotions may be in pain at times, and suffer persecution, I will declare boldly that God's word is true.

God's power is within us. God has invested Himself in us.

2 Corinthians 4:7 KJV
But we have <u>this treasure in earthen vessels</u>, that the excellency of <u>the power</u> may be of God, and not of us.

God will see that His word is accomplished in whatever area or aspect of our lives that is lacking or failing to produce his glory. God wants his glory [his manifested presence], to be presented to the world. We are the vessels He has chosen.

Every demon force, all principalities and powers must bow at the name of Jesus.

Philippians 2:10-11 KJV
That at the name of Jesus every knee should bow, of things in heaven, and things in earth, and things under the earth; And that every tongue should confess that Jesus Christ is Lord, to the glory of God the Father.

Whatever strategy or attack that comes our way can, and will, be destroyed by the name and presence of Christ Jesus, who is living within us. We must know and understand that heaven has been given to us, in the name of Jesus.

So you see, church, the magnificent power and glory of his name throughout eternity; yet He said, "I magnify my word above my name" (Ps 138:2). We can trust his word; it is our life, both now and forever. All that God is, and all that His kingdom has to offer is wrapped in his word. We must know it, love it, and desire it above all. Any area of our lives that is not producing godly fruit (meaning God's character) are areas where we are not submitting and obeying God's word.

Psalm 119:9 KJV
Where withal shall a young man <u>cleanse his way</u>? By taking heed thereto <u>according to thy word</u>.

All dark paths, dark thoughts, and dark emotions will be cleansed and brought to the light *as we submit to God's word.*

Psalm 119:45 KJV
And I will walk at liberty: for I seek thy precepts.

All of God's ways and paths will produce liberty and freedom in our life. Even though our flesh and mind will resist, we must keep pursuing God's path. Liberty will be the end result.

No matter what affliction or persecution that sneaks up on us, God's word will give us life and comfort.

Psalm 119:50 KJV
This is my comfort in my affliction: for thy word hath quickened me.

God's word will allow us to make wise decisions. It will cause us to be successful in all of life's endeavors, and He will give us the right mental concepts to get our jobs done.

Psalm 119:98-100 KJV
Thou, through thy commandments, hast made me <u>wiser</u> than mine enemies: for they are ever with me. <u>I have more understanding</u> than all my teachers: for thy testimonies is my meditation. I understand more than the ancients, <u>because I keep thy precepts</u>.

Psalm 119:105 KJV
Thy word *is* a lamp unto my feet, and a light unto my path.

Psalm 119:130 KJV
The entrance of thy words giveth light; it giveth understanding unto the simple.

All the darkness in our lives, which is any area where the kingdom of God is not being manifested, must be submitted in all humbleness of heart to the word of God. If you don't know what the word says about your circumstances, then you should pray and seek God's face. He will reveal it to you. As we have seen, God has invested Himself in our hearts. He will not allow us to be dominated by "the snake that roars" unless we choose not to believe or obey his word. It is our choice, not his. Seek His light and truth.

No sin from the past, present or future can keep you in bondage if you will only believe and obey God's word.

Psalm 119:133 KJV
Order my steps in thy word: and let not any iniquity have dominion over me.

We have seen from the beginning of creation that God's word is final authority in all things; it is still the same today. Nothing can hold us back from our destiny if we stand in the authority of God's word and anointing.

James 4:7 KJV
Submit yourselves therefore to God. Resist the devil, and he will flee from you.

By submitting to the word, setting aside your feelings, your thoughts, your emotions, and your opinions, you shall keep your foot upon the head of "the snake that roars." You should say: "I trust you Lord. I might not understand, but I choose your word. It is final authority in my life."

Now that we have discovered God's word, let us walk in it. Amen ["So be it"].

— Part B —

Being Established

We must now learn how to be established in the truth that God has birthed within us. We must learn to live by the word of God which has been planted in our hearts. We must be rooted and built up on the foundation of Jesus Christ and his shed blood.

We must understand that God is working in our hearts and lives, trying to conform us to his word.

Philippians 1:6
Being confident of this very thing, that he which hath begun a good work in you will perform it until the day of Jesus Christ.

The work that God is performing in our lives is according to, and directed by, the word of God that we have recognized and received.

We are a new creation that never existed before.

2 Corinthians 5:17
Therefore if any man be in Christ, he is <u>a new creature</u>: old things are passed away; behold, all things are become new.

We were born again—meaning that God, by the seed of his word, gave eternal life to the natural spirit within us. The natural spirit within us was dead to the life of God, and needed to be recreated to house the eternal Sprit of God.

1 Peter 1:23
Being born again, not of corruptible seed, but of incorruptible, by the word of God, which liveth and abideth for ever.

In the natural, we are the fruit of our father's sperm and mother's egg. Our distinguishing traits [such as of personality] are inherited characteristics from our parents. However, now we are the fruit of our *spiritual* seed and have the character of our Father in Heaven manifested in our life.

Hebrews 12:9
Furthermore we have had fathers of our flesh which corrected us, and we gave them reverence: shall we not much rather be in subjection unto the Father of spirits, and live?

We can only be in subjection to our Spiritual Father one way—by faith ["Father Always In The Heart"]. Since we are aware that God is truly living within us, faith should not be considered as an unattainable thing. God corrects and instructs us in one manner only: by His word. His word expels and exposes all rebellion that might be within us.

Hebrews 11:6
But without faith it is impossible to please him: for he that cometh to God must believe that he is, and that he is a rewarder of them that diligently seek him.

Without faith ("<u>F</u>ather always <u>i</u>n <u>t</u>he <u>h</u>eart") it is <u>impossible</u> [no other way] to please God. We are incapable of pleasing God by any other method. God rewards those who seek him diligently—which means to seek him in a steady, earnest, and energetic effort.

We enter into a relationship with God through and by the word. Our union with our Father began in faith, simply believing His word. So we must *continue* our relationship in the same manner.

Romans 10:8-10 NIV
But what does it say? "The word is near you; it is in your mouth and in your heart," that is, the message concerning <u>faith</u> that we proclaim: If you declare with your mouth, "Jesus is Lord," and believe in your heart that God raised him from the dead, you will be saved.

For it is with your <u>heart</u> that <u>you believe</u> and are justified, and it is with your <u>mouth</u> that <u>you profess your</u> faith and are saved.

So, we can clearly see that our spiritual life is born by receiving, believing, and saying the word of God. Our heart directs our mouth to speak the ways and thoughts of God.

We begin our life by the Living Word, Christ Himself. He established us with his word and will continue to consistently maintain our lives by His word.

Hebrews 12:2
Looking unto Jesus <u>the author and finisher of our faith</u>; who for the joy that was set before him endured

the cross, despising the shame, and is set down at the right hand of the throne of God.

We are established [to institute permanently, being a law within us] by seeking, receiving, and believing the word of God.

Just as newborn babies desire [crave] food to nourish and grow by, we must desire the word.

1 Peter 2:2
As newborn babes, desire the sincere milk of the word, that ye may grow thereby.

The milk of God's word will mature and sustain us until we are able to receive the meat of His word.

1 Corinthians 3:2
I have fed you with milk, and not with meat: for hitherto ye were not able *to* bear it, neither yet now are ye able.

We have to grow up spiritually, and be mature men and women of God. Only as we are able to receive and understand God's word, He will then reveal Himself more and more to us.

1 Corinthians 3:1
And I, brethren, could not speak unto you as unto spiritual, but as unto carnal, even as unto babes in Christ.

We must walk in the light that we already have in order to receive more light. The light gets stronger and stronger, the closer we get to Him. There is only one way that we can mature and not remain babies in Christ. To do so, we must be quick to repent and obey as He speaks to us. If we do not grow as spiritual sons and daughters, we will remain carnal, in other words, controlled by our flesh, not our spirit.

Matthew 5:6
Blessed are they which do hunger and thirst after righteousness: for they shall be filled.

The word of God is our meat, our milk, and our bread. The seed of the word of God is planted in our hearts (our spirits), and that seed reproduces itself within our life's arena. As we can see from the verse above, there is a blessing for those of us who will hunger and thirst after righteousness [right standing] with our Father.

Jesus also referred to God's word as "meat."

John 4:32
But he said unto them, I have meat to eat that ye know not of.

The meat of God's word will reveal His plan and purpose for our lives. Most of the time, our friends and family will not understand the meat of God's word for our personal lives. We must continue in obedience to His word spoken to us. In His timing, He will confirm His presence, plan, and purpose in our lives.

John 4:34
Jesus saith unto them, My meat is to do the will of him that sent me, and to finish his work.

We must do as Jesus did; meaning, we must recognize God has a will and plan for our life. This is our priority. Anything else is second in comparison to the will of God.

We are to live a life in agreement with, and under the authority of, God's word. We must realize His great love for us. This will enable us to believe that the same Spirit that dwells in Christ, also dwells within us, causing us to be like Him.

We must feed our spiritual man so that he is strong and in control of our lives by the power of the Holy Spirit and the word of God.

Luke 4:4

And Jesus answered him, saying, It is written, That man shall not live by bread alone, but by every word of God.

Remember, what you don't feed dies! Our "old" man (our natural man) is dead in Christ. Our life now is a spiritual life, which is fed with spiritual food that has been anointed by God. God intends for our inner man to be submitted to His Spirit. God's Spirit should be in complete authority over all that pertains to our life.

Romans 6:6

Knowing this, that <u>our old man is crucified with him</u>, that the body of sin might be destroyed, that henceforth we should not serve sin.

Let the old man remain dead; leave him in the grave! Don't feed him anything; he's *dead*. In our natural bodies, we determine how we grow and maintain our health by what we eat and drink—by what we put in our body. Likewise, in regards to our spiritual bodies, we must put into our spirit the food that *it* grows by—the word of God. We need to seek God daily for his bread (his word) that we need for all the aspects of our life.

Luke 11:3
Give us day by day our daily bread.

We need a vibrant relationship with God, our Father, through Jesus Christ. The term "vibrant" means "pulsating with vigor and activity." We should fellowship daily in his word, prayer, and His presence. If we do, our spirit man will be strong, healthy, and in control of our lives. We need God's word daily. In our everyday consumption of God's word, we are not only taking care of the now, but are also making provision for our future. Jesus said that he was the spiritual food we need.

John 6:48
I am that bread of life.

Jesus is the substance of our daily lives. Whatever need we have occurring each day, He is the provision for that. We must be willing at all times to eat of His flesh (bread) and drink of His blood (life). Even though our flesh and mind wants to draw back, we must remember our life is in the living word (Christ).

John 6:51
I am the living bread which came down from heaven: if any man eat of this bread, he shall live for ever: and the bread that I will give is my flesh, which I will give for the life of the world.

John 6:55-56
For my flesh is meat indeed, and my blood is drink indeed. He that eateth my flesh, and drinketh my blood, dwelleth in me, and I in him.

So, we can see that a healthy and victorious Christian life can only be obtained and maintained by feeding ourselves with the word of God. God's word is alive and contains the power within itself to mold and conform us into the image of Christ.

Studying and obeying God's word is the only way to be approved by him.

2 Timothy 2:15
Study to show thyself approved unto God, a workman that needeth not to be ashamed, rightly dividing the word of truth.

Studying will cause us to be a workman that needeth not to be ashamed. Spending time in God's word will give us the ability to rightly divide the Scriptures and to appropriate that truth as it pertains to the circumstances we are dealing with.

God's word is the answer, the solution, to any circumstance, calamity, distress, or misfortune that comes into our lives.

Hebrews 4:12
For the word of God is quick, and powerful, and sharper than any two-edged sword, piercing even to the dividing asunder of soul and spirit, and of the joints and marrow, and is a discerner of the thoughts and intents of the heart.

His word is the measuring stick with which we identify the source of everything that comes into our lives. The word reveals and analyzes all situations that could affect our lives.

We must let the word of God change our thoughts, our emotions, and our actions, so that our decisions will be subject to the word.

Romans 12:2
And be not conformed to this world [Stop being jammed into this world mold] but be ye transformed, [metamorphosed] by the renewing of your mind, that ye may prove what is the good, and acceptable and perfect will of God.

Our spirit, or our inner man, is changed immediately when we accept Christ. Our thought-life and emotions must be transformed from fleshly 'carnal' thoughts to accepting the idea that we should see ourselves as God sees us. We discover this as we seek and search out God's word.

Ephesians 2:2-3
Wherein in times past ye walked according to the curse of this world, according to the prince of the power of the air [the snake that roars], the Spirit that now worketh in the children of disobedience among whom also we all had our conversation [manner of life] in times past in the lusts of our flesh, fulfilling the desires of the flesh [five senses] and of the mind [will, intellect and emotions] and were by nature the children of wrath, even as others.

When we were born again we became new creatures in Christ. Up until that time, we had lived our lives anyway we wanted. Our decisions, concepts, opinions and moral judgments were based on the world system. Whatever was popular, whatever was accepted, the newest trend, was our measuring stick. But now, children of God, our measuring stick is the principles, the ordinances, the statutes, and the truth of the word of God.

Our mind can only be changed as we take in new information, new principles, new ideas, new precepts, and new concepts. As God's word comes into our mind little by little, our thinking changes. When our thinking changes, our behavior changes.

We must have the same attitude of the heart, to be ready at all times, in any circumstance, to search the Scriptures before making any judgments or decisions that affect our lives, and the lives of our loved ones.

Acts 17:11
These were more noble than those in Thessalonica, in that they received the word with readiness of mind, and <u>searched the scriptures daily</u>, whether these things were so.

We need to learn to overcome our flesh, as its desires are not usually good for us.

Romans 7:18
For I know that in me [that is, in my flesh] dwelleth no good thing, for to will is present with me, but how to perform that which is good I find not.

The flesh encompasses the five senses: hearing, seeing, touching, smelling, and tasting. We cannot overcome our fleshly desires (control our flesh) with any natural means or weapons, nor by our own will power. Even though we want to do well, and succeed, we simply cannot do it in our own strength or power. The flesh wants what it wants—when it wants it! We are accustomed to giving in to our fleshly desires, even if it leads to our own destruction. Our answer and our strength to overcoming all failure is knowing who we are in Christ.

Ephesians 6:12
For we wrestle not against flesh and blood, but against principalities, against powers, against the rules of the darkness of this world, against spiritual wickedness in high places.

The snake that roars [Satan] is behind all the principalities and darkness that comes against our hearts and minds. Our heart and spirit is God's arena. As I have said, 'heart' is the spiritual ear. God leads us, speaks to us, and reveals himself in our heart, not our flesh. When our mind is renewed and transformed, it is in unity with our spirit. The flesh is no match for the mind and spirit controlled by the word of God.

Ephesians 4:23
And be renewed in the spirit of your mind.

As the Scriptures consistently show us, when we are saved, it is our spirit that is born anew, but our mind is in the same condition, filled with whatever information we have allowed to be put into it. Now, all that thinking must be changed to God's thoughts and ways; therefore, making our life worth living.

2 Corinthians 4:16
For which cause we faint not, but though our outward man perish, yet the inward man is renewed day by day.

We have choices to make every day under all kinds of circumstances and situations. We can be victorious even though the outward circumstances may look dark and evil. All the wisdom, strength, and courage we need for any situation is within our heart. Remember, God is living within us!

Ephesians 4:1-18
This I say therefore, and testify in the Lord, that ye henceforth [from now on] walk not as other Gentiles walk in the vanity [depravity, futility] of their mind. Having their understanding darkened, being alienated from the life of God [His word] through the ignorance that is in them, because of the blindness of the heart.

Even though we are born again as new creatures in Christ, if we do not renew our minds and change our thought life [our soulish man] we will have a continuous roller coaster ride in our mind. Our soul, which is our mind, as well as our will, and our intellect, must learn to rely, trust and depend on the word or God as our one and only source of life.

James 1:24
Wherefore lay apart all filthiness and superfluity [excess, naughtiness, disobedience, misbehavior] and receive the engrafted [implanted] word which is able to save [to change] your soul.

God loves us so much! We are His children; we have become one of His very own who has been bought with His own blood. He has provided all that we need to have a loving personal relationship with Him. As He reveals Himself to us in His word, we can see all of our imperfections, hang-ups, etc., which we need to get rid of. All of these things are avenues which the enemy can use against us.

1 Corinthians 6:20
For ye are bought with a price; therefore glorify God in your body, and in your spirit, which are Gods.

We are redeemed with the precious blood of Jesus. When we receive that truth in the depths of our hearts, we will realize the great love that our heavenly Father has for us. With that love being such a reality to us, we will surrender all that we are to Him.

Ephesians 1:6
To the praise of the glory of His grace, wherein He hath made us accepted in the beloved.

God's grace, being much more than just favor, is truly Him revealing His ability in our lives. God deals with us as His beloved children. He doesn't reveal all our faults and failures at once, but little by little as our love and trust grows for Him, He will reveal the stumbling blocks in our lives. Satan will take advantage of any and all darkness in our lives.

Exodus 23:30
By little and little I will drive them out from before them [our enemies, all darkness in our spirit] until they be increased and inherit the land.

God wants to give us our spiritual inheritance, which is a land flowing with milk and honey. All of the light and truth in God's word always exposes any darkness in our lives. God lives and walks in the light; whereas Satan can only survive in darkness and deceit.

Isaiah 28:9-10
When shall He teach knowledge? And when shall He make to understand doctrine [the message] that are weaned from the milk and drawn from the breast. For precept [a command or principle intended as a general rule of action or conduct] must be upon precept; line upon line upon line; here a little and there a little.

So, as we see my brothers and sisters, God wants us to seek Him concerning all things that pertain to our lives. Nothing is too small or too big for our Heavenly Father. If it matter to us, it matters to Him. He will not overwhelm us. In His steadfast love and faithfulness towards us, He will reveal His word which will always deliver us out of darkness into His marvelous light.

The mind is the gateway into the spirit and heart; that is why the mind must be renewed.

Colossians 3:10
And have put on the new man which is <u>renewed in knowledge</u> after the image of Him that created Him.

We, as born-again children of God, are created in His image and likeness. God is a Spirit, and we are spiritual beings. Therefore, we must learn and grow within our spirits, as that is who we really are.

Titus 3:5
Not by works of righteousness which we have done, but according to His mercy He saved us, by the washing of regeneration and renewing of the Holy Ghost.

Our minds are the key to the opening up of the kingdom of God within us. If we fail to renew our mind, we will remain a slave to the God of this world—which is the snake that roars. Satan keeps us as his slaves through lies, deceit, and counterfeiting the things of God.

2 Corinthians 4:3-4
But our Gospel be hid [veiled], it is hidden to them that are lost [not walking in the light]; in whom the god of this world hath blinded the minds of them which believe not, lest the light of the glorious Gospel of Christ, who is the image of God, should shine unto them.

Satan is always attempting to enter our minds, to derail our intentions, and to distract us from our purposes and plans for a godly life. He will use any avenue or method to change our thought life in ways which will cause us to accept or reject the plans of God.

When we believe and speak the word of God we have the mind of the Spirit and the mind of Christ, which are one in the same. God's word and presence will always bring peace to the heart.

Daniel 26:3
Thou wilt keep him in perfect peace, whose mind [will, intellect, emotions] is stayed on thee: because he trusted in Thee.

Even in the midst of chaos and confusion, we can have peace within. The peace within our hearts acts as an umpire in our lives. The umpire calls the shots.

1 Corinthians 2:16
For who hath known the mind of the Lord, that he may instruct Him? But we have the mind of Christ.

Our thoughts, our opinions, our believe system, and our moral values will produce from the seeds that have been sown into it. We must be certain that all of these avenues are sown from God's word.

Proverbs 23:7
For as he thinketh in his heart, so is he.

So, we see that the truth in the heart makes you who you are. You may say and do many things, but the truth within your heart will determine the outcome of your life.

Romans 8:5-6
For they that after the flesh do mind the things of the flesh; but they that are after the Spirit the things of the Spirit. For to be carnal [relating to or given to sensual pleasures and appetites] is death [no life concerning the things of God] but to be spiritually minded is life and peace.

Whatever you spend your time thinking about will determine the path that you will walk. If you choose the spiritual way, God's presence and character will be manifested in your life. If you choose the fleshly life, you will be at the mercy of all their rules, regulations, and outcomes.

Romans 8:7-8
Because the carnal mind is at enmity [hostile] against God; for it is not subject to the law of God, neither indeed can be. So then they that are in the flesh [controlled by the flesh] cannot please God.

Our flesh wants what it wants and it wants it now! Satan attacks the weaknesses of our flesh with intruding and tormenting thoughts. Fear is the opposite of faith. Fear is the emotion the enemy uses to steal our faith. The only way to please God is to live a life with its roots in His word.

1 Corinthians 10:13
There hath no temptation taken you but such is common to man; but God is faithful who will not suffer [permit] you to be tempted above that [tested] ye are able, but will with the temptations also a way to escape that ye be able to bear it.

There are no temptations or desires that can overcome you if you seek God with all of your heart and follow the instructions that He reveals to your spirit. God will not allow you to be controlled and manipulated by Satan if He is on the throne of your heart.

Mark 14:38
Watch ye and pray, lest ye enter into temptation. The spirit truly is ready, but the flesh is weak.

Our answer is in our prayer life. We must keep an open heart with daily communication with the Lord. All failures in our life will be prayer failures. Our prayer life keeps our relationship with the Lord new and fresh. When these onslaughts and tormenting thoughts come, and they surely will, know and believe that your prayers will keep the enemy at bay.

Our prayers, which are based on God's word, will not only stop our spiritual enemies but will, in fact, alter our plans and decisions in regards to God's plan. Our mind is the deciding factor as to the quality and quantity of our natural lives. Our minds should be changed according to the spiritual truths as God reveals them in our heart.

Colossians 1:21
And you, that were sometime [once] alienated and enemies in your mind by wicked works, yet now hath He reconciled.

If we allow Satan access to our minds through his deception and lies, our very own mind will become an enemy to the word of God. What we read, see, and listen to can, and will, literally deceive our minds. Our mind truly is the initial battleground of the enemy. Whatever information we allow into our minds will determine our attitudes and decisions. It will certainly alter our personalities.

If we only hear the word of God without obeying, we are deceiving ourselves.

James 1:22

But be ye doers of the word, and not hearers only, deceiving your own selves.

The word of God is our only true light in this life's journey. Satan's main objective is to keep us unaware of God's word for our life. If he can do this with his deceit and lies, we will remain in darkness with a bitter, unfruitful spiritual life.

James 1:25

But whoso looketh into the perfect law of liberty continues [remains] therein, he being not a forgetful hearer, but a doer of the work; this man shall be blessed in his deed.

We must have an obedient servant's heart to quickly recognize and obliterate [to remove from our memory] all tormenting thoughts that are not submitted to the word of God. All fear has torment [severe suffering or anguish]; fear is not from our Father but from THE SNAKE THAT ROARS! God promises that we will be blessed – yielding forth productive fruit in all the areas of our life when we obey the word.

1 John 4:18

There is no fear in love, but perfect love casteth out fear, because fear hath torment; he that feareth is not made perfect [mature or complete] in love.

Satan wants to inject fears into our mind, for example, a fear such as God does not love us because we are unworthy. Satan's words are not true! My brothers and sisters, all he speaks are lies! When we submit all thoughts to the word of God, God's love grows within us and within our hearts. When we truly realize how great God's love is for us, fear cannot remain a deciding factor in our lives. He loves us not based on what we do, but on the fact that we have been accepted by his beloved son. With that always in mind, it is more easily understood that His love is already in us.

1 John 2:5
But whoso keepeth His word, in him verily [truly] is the love of God perfected [matured]. Hereby know we that we are in Him.

It is very simply stated that when we obey God's word, that in itself causes his love to mature in us. God and his word are one. When we are full of the word, we are full of God, Himself. Christ is the Living Word, living in each and every born-again Christian.

1 John 4:8
…God is love.

Love is who God is; love is what He is. His love dictates and controls all things pertaining to our life. God's love is not going to change towards us. There is nothing, nor anyone, that can cause God to change his love for us. The only person, place or thing that can change our standing before God is us!

Ephesians 2:4
But God, who is rich in mercy, for His great love wherewith He loved us.

We must not let our mind be carried away from all that God has for us, which is our inheritance that his great love has provided. His love is not like what mankind calls "love," which changes with a drop of a hat or with our emotional ups and downs. His love is both steadfast and eternal.

All of God's promises to us are always true whether we are walking and abiding in them or not.

2 Corinthians 1:20 NIV
For no matter how many promises God has made, they are "Yes" in Christ. And so through him the "Amen" ["it is so"] is spoken by us to the glory of God.

God, himself, wants his word to be manifested in our lives. When this is so, we walk in freedom and victory and he gets glory.

2 Corinthians 7:1
Dearly beloved, let us <u>cleanse ourselves</u> from all filthiness of the flesh and spirit, perfecting holiness in the fear [reverence] of God.

Notice, church, that we are to do this cleaning up. This is done by the choice we make of casting down all thoughts and emotions that do not line up with the word of God. We are to be quick to recognize any darkness or failures in our life that results in an unfruitful spiritual life. We must seek God with a loving servant's heart for direction and exposure so that the enemy can be stopped in his maneuvers.

2 Corinthians 10:5-6

Casting down imaginations and every high [proud] thing that exalted itself against the knowledge of God and bringing into captivity every thought to the obedience of Christ. And having in a readiness to revenge [to punish] all disobedience when your obedience is fulfilled.

No one, not even God Himself, can stop our thoughts—*but we can!* But it is only by our choice to do so. In order to change our thoughts, we must replace them with the word of God. We must choose to change our "stinkin' thinkin'," our old ways of receiving and responding to thoughts that enter our mind. We must be willing to compare our thoughts to God's thoughts which will produce his character and a truly abundant life.

Our old man (with our old man's thoughts) produces death, darkness and bondage in our lives. We need to take off our grave clothes, which were appropriate for our old sin nature. Now, we are new creations in Christ Jesus with a divine nature and abilities.

John 12:43

And when He thus had spoken, He cried with a loud voice, Lazarus, come forth! And he that was dead came forth, bound hand and foot in grave clothes; and his face was bound with a napkin. Jesus saith into them "Loose [unbind] him, and let him go."

Church, those words are forever true. We are to be loosed, set free, from all that binds and hinders our walk with Christ. It is the word of God that accomplishes this task. As the word of God is revealed to our spirit (our heart) and as we obey the truth, we are loosed from all darkness and deceit. God's word is intended for spiritual beings—which we are at the new birth. When that truth is spoken and received, it has the resurrection power from on high to replace darkness with life.

1 Peter 5:5
And be clothed with humility [meekness] for God resisteth the proud and giveth grace to the humble.

We are to have hearts that are humbled before God to destroy the power and prestige that our own thoughts have maintained in our life but now are being put in subjection to God's word. Not only must our mind be renewed [to make or become new] but it must establish [to institute permanently] the principles and ordinances of God's word.

To establish something in our lives is to say that it is an everyday integral [essential to completeness] behavior in our life. God established His covenant with us so that it would be with us forever. He will always and forever know and honor His covenant [agreement] with us.

Genesis 6:18
But with thee will I establish my covenant, and thou shalt come into the ark [the presence of god], thou and thy sons and thy wife and thy son's wives with thee.

All that we hold dear to our hearts, our children and grandchildren, if submitted to the word of God, will be protected, nourished and matured. Church, let us be established in God's word, in His way of thinking and doing. As we live as examples in our covenant before our children and grandchildren, these seeds will have the honor and privilege of being injected into their lives.

2 Chronicles 20:20
Believe in the Lord your God, so shall ye be established [safely kept], believe His prophets so shall ye prosper.

To be established in God's word, we must speak and declare before everyone that truly it is the deciding factor in our lives. We must prophesy to ourselves, meaning, we must speak what God's word says to us and about us. The power is in the word itself to produce the very life with which it speaks and brings forth.

Job 22:28
<u>**Thou shalt also decree [command or dictate] a thing,**</u> **and it shall be established unto thee; and the light shall shine upon they ways.**

Our hearts established in the word will cause the reality of the promise to be manifested in our flesh [our natural life]. The promise in a believing heart is greater than life, greater than the lies and deceptions of the flesh. We must always realize that words are not "just words"; they either produce life or death. With the word implanted in our heart and the Holy Spirit prompting us, we will speak life.

Psalm 112:8
His heart is established, He shall not be afraid until He sees His desire upon His enemies.

When our hearts are established in the word, we are not afraid of evil tidings or reports. An established heart will always give us the victory over our enemies. When our hearts are full to overflowing with God's principles and ordinances, our hearts will never be afraid of evil reports but will, in truth, know that God's spoken word in our mouth will prevail.

Proverbs 16:7
When a man's [mankind] ways please the Lord, He maketh his enemies to be at peace with him.

Brothers and sisters, how do we please God? How marvelous are His ways! Oh, the simplicity of His truth! We please Him by having faith in His word. Believing His word is the only way we can live a life pleasing in His sight. The only things we need to do are read and believe.

If you do not know the word of God, you cannot have any faith. Faith is a spiritual force fed by spiritual food—which is the word of God. Faith is not of the head, it is of the heart. You can have doubt in your thoughts, yet great faith in your heart. Do not speak the doubt, but rather, speak the word—which equals faith.

Hebrews 11:6
But without faith it is impossible to please Him; for he that cometh to God must believe that He is.

As I have said before, faith is remembering:

F – Father
A – Always
I – In
T – The
H – Heart

God's Spirit, His truth, His anointing, and His consecration have been done in our hearts. He is, therefore, within our heart for all eternity—now and forever. Our part of the deal is to submit our thoughts and believe His word. He will do the rest. Our part is to fight the good fight of faith [which is submitting the thoughts, emotions, and actions of our flesh, and to honor and obey his word]. He honors and bows Himself to what He has spoken (His word), and will do whatever is necessary to see that the word brings forth life and healing. God said:

Isaiah 55:11
So shall my word be that goeth forth out of my mouth; it shall not return unto me void [without results], but it shall accomplish that which I please, and it shall prosper in all the things whereto I sent it.

If our thoughts, which produce our actions, are established on the word of God, we shall not fail in any endeavor of our lives. We are established by believing and speaking the word of God. This is the only way; there is no other. God's resurrection power, and life are abiding in the written word.

Proverbs 12:17
He that speaketh truth showeth forth righteousness; but a false witness deceit.

Anything or anyone not submitted to God's word is deceitful, and we know the origin of that—the snake that roars. The truth of God's word will always lead us to Him and His ways. Righteousness in the simplest terms means that we are in right-standing with the God of the universe, our heavenly Father.

The enemy cannot overcome God's righteousness. So we must always have our heart and mouth full of the word of God.

Proverbs 12:19
The lip of truth shall be established forever: but a lying tongue is for a moment.

When our lips are speaking the truths of the word, we are being established in God's kingdom. God's kingdom has rules and regulations which are governed by the truth of the Scriptures. God's truth cannot be changed because it is connected to His changeless character.

John 17:17
Sanctify [set apart to God's thoughts and purposes] them through thy truth, thy word is truth.

We must commit our ways of doing and thinking to God's way of doing and thinking. His word, when received into our hearts, will change our attitudes, opinions, and religious perceptions. He has provided His word to teach and mold us into His very own spiritual children. God does not want us to be "religious," but rather, He wants a personal relationship with us, as a Father would desire with his very own children.

Proverbs 16:3
Commit thy works unto the Lord, and thy thoughts shall be established.

Every plan and purpose in our lives must be determined by the word of God. As we acknowledge God in all that we do daily, he will reveal His thoughts and ways to us. If it is important to us, it is important to God.

Proverbs 20:18
Every purpose is established by counsel [deliberation together; agreement with God's word]: and with good advice make war.

We must ask God to counsel our hearts regarding every situation that occurs in our life. There are many occasions in our life where we will have to fight for God's inheritance to be received into our life. This is not a natural fight with carnal weapons. We must know how to shoot the arrows of God's word. The enemy of our soul will make war with our hearts and spirits, but God's Holy Spirit will teach our hands to war.

Joshua 9:14
And the men took of their victuals [their own provisions] and asked not the counsel of God.

We cannot depend on our own strength or resources to defeat the enemy. All of our victory is in the counsel of God. The enemy will deceive you into thinking you can do it on your own; it is always a lie. Outside of God, and the truth of His word, there is no victory.

Judges 18:5
And they said unto him, ask counsel we pray thee, of God, that we may know whether our way which we go shall be prosperous.

Any decision in any area of our life's arena must be directed by the counsel of God, which is the word of God. His word will always cause us to be overcomers and prosperous in whatever we decide to do in our life.

Psalm 73:24
Thou shalt guide me with thy counsel, and afterward receive me to glory.

The glory of God is the anointing of God; therefore, the counsel of God will always be overshadowed by the Holy Ghost. God's counsel to us will produce His glory in our life.

Psalm 1:1
Blessed is the man that walketh not in the counsel of the ungodly, nor standeth in the way of sinners nor sitteth in the seat of the scornful.

Simply put, church, whatever we do, whatever concerns we might have, whether walking, standing, or sitting, we are not to receive any counsel except the word of God. So, we can see God wants us, His children, to have our hearts continually on His word and His ways.

Psalm 107:10-11
Such as sit in darkness and in the shadow of death, being bound [prisoners in affliction] and iron, because they reveled against the words of God and contemned the counsel of the Most High.

We cannot run or hide from the fact that we cannot live a victorious spiritual life outside the word of God. The "snake that roars" is always attempting to maneuver [an evasive movement or shift of tactics] or manipulate [to influence especially with intent to deceive] the affairs of our life so that we do not acknowledge or submit to the word of God. He never attacks up front, but always from behind in darkness and deceit. If we rebel against the word of God, we will remain in bondage along with the many afflictions of the enemy.

Proverbs 20:5
Counsel in the heart of man is like deep water, but a man of understanding will draw it out.

So, we can see that God wants us to receive His counsel, which is His word. He makes every attempt to get His word into our hearts. The truth is always received and revealed in our heart. When we pray and seek God's heart, He will quicken His thoughts and ways to us.

Proverbs 20:27
The spirit of man is the candle of the Lord [Jehovah] <u>searching all the inwards parts of the belly within our hearts is the life and truth of God.</u>

Our heart is where He speaks, He directs, and He comforts. All that He does is first received in our hearts and then manifested in the flesh [the natural realm]. He attempts to speak to us even in our sleep. He is continually seeking to reveal His heart to our heart.

Job 33:14-16
For God [Elohim] speaketh once, yea twice, yet man perceiveth it not, in a dream, in a vision of the night,

when deep sleep falleth upon man, in slumberings upon the bed, then he openeth the ears of man, and sealeth their instructions, that He may withdraw man from his purpose [work] and hide pride from man.

God's love is so great towards us that He never sleeps or slumbers, but is always looking for an inroad into our hearts and lives. He speaks to us in dreams at night because He wants, so very much, to reveal Himself and His word to us. We are so busy with living through the day, our minds clamoring with life's details, that He cannot get our attention. So, in our dreams at night, He can reveal His plans and purposes for our life, warning us of the enemy's attacks and wrong decisions we may make.

Psalm 16:7
I will bless the Lord, who hath given me counsel [guidance]: my reigns [mind] also instruct me in the night seasons.

God's presence is always with us, His love is overshadowing us so that He can get us to receive His truth and His blessings within our heart. So, even in the night seasons, he is looking for ways to guide and instruct us.

Psalm 51:6
Thou desireth truth in the inward parts and in the hidden part. Thou shalt make me to know wisdom.

Again, in the Scripture above, we see He is seeking to get His truth and wisdom into our hearts, which we know is our spiritual ear. The "snake that roars," in his deceit, is ever trying to get us to receive false counsel. He uses people, even our own thoughts against us, which have not been renewed by the word of God. The greatest weapon of the enemy is our lack of knowledge of the word of God, or the wrong interpretation of God's word.

Hosea 4:6
My people are destroyed for a lack of knowledge.

Church, there is no counsel, plan, or purpose that can stand against God's counsel, or His plan and purpose for you and me. We are only destroyed by not knowing or accepting the truth of God's word. His word will overcome any deceit or darkness that would attempt to take preeminence over His word.

Psalm 33:10-11
The Lord [Jehovah] bringeth the counsel of the heathen [ungodly] to naught [nothing]. He maketh the devices [plans] of the people of none effect. The counsel of the Lord [Jehovah] stands forever, the thought of His heart to all generations.

Praise God, church, that includes you and me! His heart and His counsel are for us today. There is no counsel or device that can overcome us. Anything or anyone attempting to enter our life without the limits of the word of God cannot be successful.

Proverbs 11:14
Where no counsel [guidance] is, the people fall: but in the multitudes of counselors there is safety.

We must not be "lone rangers," meaning we need the counsel of God to be communicated to us through godly people.

We cannot be left to depend on, or believe in, our own natural abilities. God has provided His word to guide us in all of life's endeavors.

Proverbs 15:22
Without counsel purposes are disappointed; but in the multitude of counselors they are established.

We must have spiritual brothers and sisters who know the word of God, and will be in agreement with us concerning God's counsel and His plan for our life. We must not be in fear or have anxiety about seeking the spiritual counselors that God would choose to minister to us.

Proverbs 19:21
There are many devices [plans] in a man's heart; nevertheless the counsel [purpose] of the Lord [Jehovah] shall stand.

All the issues of our life proceed from our heart; therefore, our only hope of receiving and walking in our godly inheritance is to have a heart full of the counsel of the word of God. Any path or plan that we take outside of God's word will not prosper. For God to prosper and bless the decisions we make, He must be part of them.

Proverbs 20:18
Every purpose is established by counsel; and with good advice make war.

This is a battle, church, but God has provided all our weapons, all the strategy that we need for a successful campaign against the snake that roars. We can shout the victory! We can exalt Him in our dance, giving Him all the glory and honor because He is our possession! He is our inheritance! He is our counsel! God's truth and counsel shall keep and protect us in all the endeavors of this life.

We have to keep our hearts and minds in a constant mode of receiving, whether in our sleep or in our waking hours, from our pastor or in a book. God uses many varied ways to get His counsel (His word) into our circumstances.

Acts 20:27
For I have not shunned [hesitated] to declare unto you all the counsel of God.

For every situation or every circumstance that we may encounter in this life, God's counsel will cause all of these to be in our favor. We cannot just accept *part* of God's counsel. He is consistently revealing His word to our life, whether in our behavior or belief system. With His word, He is changing and transforming us into His sons and daughters.

Proverbs 8:28
And we know that all things work together for good to those that love God, to them who are the called according to His purpose.

So we see, church, that God, in His awesome love for us, has determined that we shall have His abundant inheritance manifested in our lives by simply seeking out His counsel with a believing heart. His word causes all things, no matter how dark and evil it looks, to work for our good.

Hebrews 6:17-19 NIV
Because God wanted to make the unchanging nature of his purpose very clear to the heirs of what was promised, <u>he confirmed it with an oath</u>.

God did this so that, by two unchangeable things in which it is impossible for God to lie, we who have fled to take hold of the hope set before us may be greatly encouraged. We have this hope as an anchor for the soul, firm and secure. It enters the inner sanctuary behind the curtain (veil).

God's word, His counsel, removes the veil from our heart and minds, releasing us to walk into our inheritance. God made an oath that His word would keep us, protect us, and deliver us from anything the enemy may throw at us. His word is truly our refuge and hope. God's counsel will always produce peace in our mind and emotions, causing us to rest in His presence. Praise God! Hallelujah! The snake that roars is a defeated foe!

— Part C —

Consistently Maintaining

We have seen through our Father's word, our beginning in Him; also, we are to be established in His principles and statutes. Now, we will discover together how our Father also provided for us a way to maintain this new life, with Him receiving all of the glory. We must allow God's word and counsel to promote His character and kingdom in our daily lives.

Galatians 4:19
My little children, of whom I travail in birth again until Christ be formed in you.

We must consistently, through heart-felt prayer, seek God. We must allow the Holy Spirit to reveal areas in our life which are not submitted to the word of God. Because we are not submitted, we do not have victory, and God's glory is not manifested in our life. God's correcting hand is always motivated by love. Love never fails us.

As we present ourselves to be conformed to God's word we will always be established and maintained in our spiritual inheritance. God's kingdom is revealed to our hearts as we prayerfully seek His face and wisdom. The Lord wants to establish us in His truth, not only for our benefit, but for those who we come in contact with in our daily lives.

Philippians 1:6
Being confident of this very thing, that He which hath began a good work in you will perform [continue, complete] it until the day of Jesus Christ.

Our Father will not give up on us; He will not forget us, nor leave us at the mercy of "the snake that roars." God will always be seeking us out to reveal Himself and His truth to our circumstances, whatever they may be. Even when our circumstances seem to be opposite of the word of God, by His spirit and truth God is working in the spiritual realm so that the end result of truth will be made known in our natural life.

2 Chronicles 16:9
For the eyes of the Lord [Jehovah] roam to and fro, throughout the whole earth, to show Himself strong in behalf of them whose heart is perfect toward Him...

Brothers and sisters, we must receive and recognize God's grace [His ability] in our lives. It truly is His power and ability within us that keeps and protects us. His grace, in effect, is His word. You cannot separate the two. God's grace is the power within His own word to produce itself in our lives. If we choose to turn away or neglect His word, there will be continual turmoil in our lives.

Colossians 1:27
To whom God would make known what is the riches of the glory of this mystery [not revealed] among the Gentiles, which is Christ in you, the hope of glory.

God's spirit is within each and every one of His children; that is where the power, the anointing, the glory is abiding. We need never worry or be concerned about any issue in our life. We must depend [rely and trust] on the abiding life of Christ within us. If we do not allow this truth and power to fight our battles, we will be continually at war. We cannot depend or trust in our own flesh [the strength of our own arm].

2 Chronicles 32:8

With him is an arm of flesh, but with us is the Lord [Jehovah] our God [Elohim] to help us, and to fight our battles and the people rested themselves [relied] upon the words of Hezekiah, King of Judea.

When we rely, trust, and depend on God's word, He will show Himself mighty and strong on our behalf. "The snake that roars" is a defeated foe which continually attempts to get us to trust in our own wisdom and ability. He knows that the flesh and emotions of our natural man is weak and easily swayed and deceived.

Psalm 89:21-11

With whom My hand shall be established; my arm also shall strengthen him. The enemy shall not exact upon him, nor do the sons of wickedness afflict him.

God wants us to believe and trust His word, we are to seek it above all else. When we recognize and understand that our strength and victory is only obtained by abiding in God's word, we will have a strong craving and desire for the truth.

Psalm 147:10
He delighteth not in the strength of the horse. He taketh not pleasure in the legs of man.

In every situation that comes against us, we must reach out and receive His word—*which is backed by all heaven itself.* God, Himself, is revealed in us when we allow His power and presence to perform His word. God takes no pleasure or acknowledgment of anything that has its origins in the flesh.

Isaiah 55:10-11
For as the rain cometh down, and the snow from heaven, and returneth not thither [there], but watereth the earth and maketh it bring forth and bud, that it may give seed to the sower and bread to the eater.
So shall <u>my word</u> be that goeth forth out of my mouth, <u>it shall not return unto me void</u> [without result], but it shall accomplish that which I do please, and it shall prosper in the thing whereto I send it.

God's word is our life-line; His words keep us in a place of hearing and receiving His promises. What the word speaks is what God speaks. He and His word are one; you cannot separate them. The Holy Spirit, the glory of God, is the power that "executes" God's word, and sees to it that it is put completely into effect. God, Himself, declares what His word will accomplish, or bring to pass, causing fruit to be produced in whatever area it is sent.

There is a planting of the seed, God's word, in our hearts. Then there is a time of watering, which is done with prayer and thanksgiving in His presence. Lastly, there comes a harvest, meaning the word spoken will produce that truth.

Psalm 138:2
I will worship toward thy holy temple, and praise thy name for thy loving kindness and for thy truth: <u>for thou hast magnified thy word above all thy name</u>.

God has surely declared that He has magnified His own word above His name. So, surely we can see that His word must be the center and priority of our lives. God, in His Holy presence, will see to it that His word will be confirmed and honored in our life.

Genesis 15:1
After these things the <u>word of the LORD</u> came unto Abram in a vision, saying, Fear not, Abram: I am thy shield, and <u>thy exceeding great reward</u>.

All of our spiritual progress and victories start with a word from God. To consistently maintain our victory and progress we must always seek God's will and counsel, which are found in His word. That counsel can come many different ways, but the word of God is the source.

God can speak to us in a dream, a vision, the written word, or a rhema word. He can also speak to us by an inward witness within our spirit (our heart).

Job 33:14-17
For <u>God speaketh</u> once, yea twice, yet man perceiveth it not. <u>In a dream</u>, in a vision of the night, when deep sleep falleth upon men, <u>in slumberings upon the bed</u>; <u>Then he openeth the ears of men, and sealeth their instruction</u>, That he may withdraw man from his purpose, and hide pride from man.

God's principles never change; maybe the way they are delivered or received change, but never the principle, itself.

Malachi 3:6
For I am the LORD, I change not...

As always, "the snake that roars" has perverted and counterfeited God's own chosen way of communication. God wants to communicate with us; He wants his message of life to be delivered to His children.

Do you not know that our covenant from Almighty God was revealed and received in a dream? God has always chosen dreams to reveal His thoughts and ways to us. He is still doing this today. We are spiritual beings, with a spiritual Father who has chosen to reveal secrets to our spirit while we are sleeping.

Genesis 15:12-14
And when the sun was going down, <u>a deep sleep fell upon Abram</u>; and, lo, an horror of great darkness fell upon him. <u>And he (God) said unto Abram</u>, Know of a surety that thy seed shall be a stranger in a land that is not theirs, and shall serve them; and they shall afflict them four hundred years; And also that nation, whom they shall serve, will I judge: and afterward shall they come out with great substance.

God is speaking to Abram about his future and his children's future. He gave him direction and knowledge that not only affected his life, but also generations to come. God is no respecter of persons; He will also speak to us in dreams when there are adversaries and situations which we are not aware of.

There are always victories and blessings contained in God's revelations to us.

Genesis 15: 17-18
And it came to pass, that when the sun when down, it was dark, behold a smoking furnace, and a burning lamp that pass between those pieces. In that same day, the Lord made a covenant with Abraham, Unto thy seed have I given this land, from the river of Egypt unto that great river, the river Euphrates.

So we see, God is declaring His covenant in a dream. He is telling Abraham all of his plans and purposes for mankind. All of Abraham's future is being detailed and revealed in a dream. So, brothers and sisters, do not take God's dreams lightly; take them before His throne, seeking His revelation.

Genesis 17:18
And Abraham said unto God, O that Ishmael might live before thee!

Abraham, in response to God's dream, is seeking His revelation and interpretation as to how it pertains in his life. Do not attempt to put a natural interpretation into a spiritual truth. God's dreams are always to impart spiritual wisdom and direction into our lives. He will use a natural picture to depict a spiritual truth.

Genesis 2:21-22
And the LORD God caused a deep sleep to fall upon Adam, and he slept: and he took one of his ribs, and closed up the flesh instead thereof; And the rib, which

the LORD God had taken from man, made he a woman, and brought her unto the man.

Church, do not let "the snake that roars" deceive or rob you of this wonderful way that He chose to reveal Himself to us. God can warn us, protect us, and give us His wisdom in dreams of the night. We can also receive our spiritual gifts and callings from God in a dream. God's spiritual truth revealed in dreams will close up all of the attempts of the flesh to have priority in our life.

1 Kings 5:3-4
Thou knowest how that David my father could not build an house unto the name of the Lord his God for the wars which were about him on every side, until the Lord put them under the soles of his feet.
But now the Lord my God hath given me rest on every side, so that there is neither adversary nor evil occurrent.

There are many areas and ways that the enemy seeks an entrance into our lives. Spiritual truth and knowledge in God's word gives us rest and protection from the enemy. He will show us in a dream, when and how the enemy will attack us.

1 Kings 3:5-14
In Gibeon <u>the Lord appeared</u> to Solomon <u>in a dream</u> by night...

God is no respecter of persons. What He did for Solomon, He will do for us. Whatever information or direction we need for a victorious spiritual life, God will see that we get it, no matter what avenue he uses to impart that information. That information is not limited to only our spiritual life, but it also covers our natural lives with whatever decisions we need to make. When we do choose God's ways and thoughts, our natural lives are sure to be blessed.

Acts 10:34
Then Peter opened his mouth, and said, Of a truth I perceive that God is no respecter of persons.

He is a respecter of His word. God also respects a heart that truly seeks and rests in His promises. Our Father seeks out those who truly love Him and wants to be transformed into His likeness. So, we need not be concerned about prestige and prominence as to our natural abilities, but only how much we are trusting and living in God's word.

2 Chronicles 16:9
For the eyes of the LORD run to and fro throughout the whole earth, to show Himself strong in the behalf of them whose heart is perfect toward him. Herein thou hast done foolishly: therefore from henceforth thou shalt have wars.

Church, we should have a heart that is perfect toward Him, wanting His truth at any cost to the flesh. As we have studied in the former section, our flesh is not subject to the law of God. Our spirit man, the hidden man of the heart, loves God's word and His counsel. Brothers and sisters, do not try to dictate to God how He will reveal Himself to you.

Do not hang on to traditions from our forefathers, whether it is grandpa or grandma. Do not let a religious spirit rob you of the true life and empowerment of the Spirit, which is rightfully yours. We can see that God says we are foolish and will continually be in a war between flesh and spirit if we are not in submission to the word of God.

Mark 7:13
Making the word of God of none effect through your tradition, which ye have delivered: and many such like things do ye.

We must let God change anything and everything in our lives that does not align itself to God's way of thinking and doing. There are attitudes and thoughts in our life which we picked up from childhood. Religion and tradition are man-made, but spiritual truth and life proceed from our heavenly Father.

Colossians 2:8
Beware lest any man spoil you through philosophy and vain deceit, after the tradition of men, after the rudiments of the world, and not after Christ.

We are to be so dependent on God's word and counsel for life that we must have our heart alert to receive His truth in any way He should decide to deliver it. By this, I mean reading the word, praying, reading spiritual books, listening to spiritual CD's and tapes, listening to our pastor or Christian television.

We must not forget receiving dreams and visions, or a word of knowledge, or word of wisdom from one of God's ministers. However, we receive the truth for one purpose: to reveal Jesus the Christ to ourselves first, and then to a dying world, so that we, ourselves, are set free from all bondage to serve Him and then reach out to others.

We cannot minister truth and freedom to someone else if it is not manifested in our own life. God loves us so much that He will go to great lengths to get His truth into our heart. When we encounter hardships, snares, or blockages in our daily path—and we will—we must cry out to the living God with a love for the truth. He will surely answer, for His glory and great namesake are at risk.

Proverbs 11:21
Though hand join in hand, the wicked shall not be unpunished: but the seed of the righteous shall be delivered.

God simply declares that our seed, our children, shall be delivered. Not might be, but **shall be** delivered. The fight for our children is not a natural fight made with natural decisions. It is a spiritual fight based on spiritual truth that will deliver.

Psalm 112:2
His seed shall be mighty upon earth: the generation of the upright shall be blessed.

Again, we see God's declaration about our seed. We must not be moved by what we see or feel, but only what the word of God says about our children. You cannot declare what you do not know.

Genesis 22:17
That in blessing I will bless thee, and in multiplying I will multiply thy seed as the stars of the heaven, and as the sand which is upon the sea shore; and thy seed shall possess the gate of his enemies.

Your children are your seed, and we are the seed of Christ, Himself, praise God! His truth, His answer will always heal, deliver, and set free. Therefore, He receives all the glory. We can also see that God said our seed would possess the gates of his enemies. That simply means that they will, by the Spirit of God, control and defeat any enemy that would destroy them [drugs, alcohol, and demon activity].

Galatians 3:16

Now to Abraham and his seed were the promises made. He saith not, And to seeds, as of many; but as of one, And to thy seed, which is Christ.

We know Christ is God's seed sown in our hearts. So, with that information, we know we are now God's seed. We are His children, born of His Spirit, as much as our children are born from our natural womb.

Galatians 3:29

And if ye be Christ's, then are ye Abraham's seed, and heirs according to the promise.

You must receive and believe God's word concerning your children. You must speak that word! Do not be moved by what you see, or by what you feel, only speak what you believe, which is God's word, His counsel concerning the matter. God will honor His word and your faith. "The snake that roars" cannot stand against God's counsel. So, if there is any issue, no matter how horrendous it appears, it can be, and will be changed by our declaring what God says about our children.

Healing belongs to you!

1 Peter 2:24
Who his own self bare our sins in his own body on the tree, that we, being dead to sins, should live unto righteousness: by whose stripes ye were healed.

The word of God has to be more real in your spirit, your heart, than the evil report of the enemy. Your flesh must not be the final say in your life; it will always say doom, gloom, and destruction. Healing belongs to you. The life of God living within you will destroy all sickness. We should eat, sleep, and pray healing scriptures.

Zephaniah 3:15
The LORD hath taken away thy judgments, he hath cast out thine enemy: the king of Israel, even the LORD, is in the midst of thee: thou shalt not see evil any more.

God's spirit is within each and everyone that belongs to Him, with all His power and glory. We must realize and believe that the power and glory that resides in us is capable of destroying all of the darkness and destruction that the enemy would deceive us with.

Colossians 1:27
To whom God would make known what is the riches of the glory of this mystery among the Gentiles; which is Christ in you, the hope of glory.

Our Father wants us healed. He wants our bodies strong and healthy. He lives there. His life is within us. There is no disease of any form or character that can withstand God's glory and power. We have only to believe his truth and great love for us. As light drives out darkness, God's life within us drives out sickness and disease. For God's life to be a full force and authority in our life, we must be solely relying and trusting in His word. The more word we have, the more power is available to us.

Psalm 103:3

Who forgiveth all thine iniquities; who healeth all thy diseases.

We can see over and over again, that God declares He has forgiven us and healed us—it is a done deal. We must override our flesh with its natural feelings, and declare that we are healed and forgiven of our sins, past and present. God's word will change the condition of our flesh and the thoughts of our hearts.

Romans 8:11

But if the Spirit of him that raised up Jesus from the dead dwell in you, he that raised up Christ from the dead shall also quicken [to restore to life] your mortal bodies by his Spirit that dwelleth in you.

God wants us to produce life and blessing in every area of our daily life. Oh my brothers and sisters, do not let "the snake that roars," with his deceit and treachery, make you believe a lie that will result in a great loss in your natural life. Our Father has not left any part of our life here on earth to chance. He has made provision for all aspects of our earthly life, including finances.

We must approach that area in our life in the same manner as with our children and our health. We must seek with humbleness of heart the whole counsel of God concerning our money matters.

First and foremost, we must be a tither, which is ten percent of our income. You might ask, "Should I tithe before taxes or after?" [I asked that question.] This is God's answer:

Matthew 22:21
They say unto him, Caesar's. Then saith he unto them, Render therefore unto Caesar the things which are Caesar's; and unto God the things that are God's.

It is really quite simple. Our taxes are not ours. They belong to the government. Now we shall see what God says about His tithe, the ten percent. We tithe only on what is ours—what we take home. Everything outside of the tithe is a gift or offering.

Malachi 3:8-14
Will a man rob God? Yet ye have robbed me. But ye say, Wherein have we robbed thee? In tithes and offerings. Ye are cursed with a curse: for ye have robbed me, even this whole nation.

Bring ye all the tithes into the storehouse, that there may be meat in mine house, and prove me now herewith, saith the LORD of hosts, if I will not open you the windows of heaven, and pour you out a blessing, that there shall not be room enough to receive it.

And I will rebuke the devourer for your sakes, and he shall not destroy the fruits of your ground; neither shall your vine cast her fruit before the time in the field,

> saith the LORD of hosts. And all nations shall call you blessed: for ye shall be a delightsome land, saith the LORD of hosts.
>
> Your words have been stout against me, saith the LORD. Yet ye say, What have we spoken so much against thee? Ye have said, It is vain to serve God: and what profit is it that we have kept his ordinance, and that we have walked mournfully before the LORD of hosts?

We must believe and receive this also into our hearts and simply obey. That old cliché "trust and obey, there is no other way," is quite simply the truth. When we have decisions to make regarding what direction we should go, whether it be concerning a job, a church, going into business, or a new location, the answer is the same: seek God with your whole heart, trusting and believing, and He will hear and answer.

God says we can, and will, fall under a curse if we do not tithe. We cannot justify in any way of not tithing. No natural circumstance can stand before God's word. We must simply love Him, trust Him, and obey Him. He will not fail us; we will walk under an open heaven—under the protection of the hedge of His word.

Deuteronomy 4:29

> But if from thence thou shalt seek the LORD thy God, thou shalt find him, if thou seek him with all thy heart and with all thy soul.

God's criterion for success in our life is to seek Him with all of our heart and soul. Our heart refers to our innermost being, and our soul refers to our mind, will, and emotions. With that yearning within our hearts, we shall surely find Him.

Psalm 138:8

The LORD will perfect that which concerneth me: thy mercy, O LORD, endureth for ever: forsake not the works of thine own hands.

So, we see all our answers and needs are to be believed and received with a humble heart before God. It is His pleasure and will to reveal Himself to His children. God will complete and mature every issue that finds its way into your life. He will never forsake us in any battle arena. We were conceived in His very own heart.

Jeremiah 33:3

Call unto me, and I will answer thee, and show thee great and mighty things, which thou knowest not.

All that our Father wants us to do is to trust Him and depend on Him as we would our earthly father in the natural sense. We must realize that His great love and faithfulness far, far outweighs the love of a natural father. We must have a willing heart that will seek Him out in all affairs of life. In doing this, we will surely receive His great mercy and His mighty works on behalf of our lives.

Galatians 4:6

And because ye are sons, God hath sent forth the Spirit of his Son into your hearts, crying, Abba, Father.

Do you see the simplicity of His truth in bringing all our cares and needs to Him? He is the source of all life. "The snake that roars" would have you believe the lie that God doesn't love you; He cannot forgive you; you're not important enough; you cannot live holy enough—*all **lies***. Satan cannot tell the truth. There is no truth in him. In truth, Abba means "daddy." The God of the universe is our very own daddy! We can enter His presence as His child, curl up on His lap, and ask anything that we need. Our daddy will love us and supply our every need.

Proverbs 3:5-6
Trust in the LORD with all thine heart; and lean not unto thine own understanding.

In all thy ways acknowledge him, and he shall direct thy paths.

Again, we see that God, our Father, has all the answers and that He wants to reveal them to us. There is only one thing that can stop us from receiving God's kingdom (which is our inheritance): an unbelieving heart that attempts to decide and direct its *own* life's plan. However, a trusting and believing heart acknowledges everything to God, and waits patiently for His wisdom.

Numbers 13:30-33
And Caleb stilled the people before Moses, and said, Let us go up at once, and possess it; for we are well able to overcome it. But the men that went up with him said, We be not able to go up against the people; for they are stronger than we.

And they brought up an evil report of the land which they had searched unto the children of Israel, saying, The land, through which we have gone to search it, is a land that eateth up the inhabitants thereof; and all the people that we saw in it are men of a great stature,

And there we saw the giants, the sons of Anak, which come of the giants: and we were in our own sight as grasshoppers, and so we were in their sight.

"The snake that roars" filled them with doubt and fear that they were the weaker ones, and were even as grasshoppers. Lies, lies, lies! Satan had them looking within their own selves, and not at what Jehovah, God, said they could do. God said it was an evil report with no truth in it. So we see, God is not pleased when we put circumstances or someone else's opinions above His word. Unbelief will always bring disaster and failure.

Proverbs 23:7
For as he thinketh in his heart, so is he: Eat and drink, saith he to thee; but his heart is not with thee.

We need not think on circumstances or the way a situation looks, but only what God has spoken to us. Real truth is only found in the heart—that is why we must continually fill our heart with God's presence and word. The truth that is within our heart is what directs our decisions, which paints the path that we walk.

Numbers 14:24
But my servant Caleb, because he had another spirit with him, and hath followed me fully, him will I bring into the land whereunto he went; and <u>his seed shall possess it.</u>

Church, this is what we want for our children and our children's children. A believing and obedient heart will leave an inheritance for children and grandchildren. We must not have an evil heart of unbelief. The truths that we believe and walk in will cause our children and grandchildren to possess the inheritance of God.

Hebrews 3:10-12
Wherefore I was grieved with that generation, and said, They do alway err in their heart; and they have not known my ways. So I sware in my wrath, They shall not enter into my rest. Take heed, brethren, lest there be in any of you an evil heart of unbelief, in departing from the living God.

So, we see again that God is not pleased with an unbelieving heart. If we do not walk in a believing and trusting heart towards God, we will never enter into the rest that He has provided for us. If we are consistently dealing with inner turmoil and the cares of this world, we are failing in believing the safety and provision of God's word.

Hebrews 3:18
And to whom sware he that they should not enter into his rest, but to them that believed not?

When we believe God and have His word in our hearts, we have a marvelous peace and rest that all is well with our souls. We cannot be moved by what we are seeing and feeling if our heart is steadfast in the truths of God. Believing God's word will truly provide a rest for our spirit and soul in the time of upheavals.

Hebrews 4:6
Seeing therefore it remaineth that some must enter therein, and they to whom it was first preached entered not in because of unbelief.

We cannot receive or maintain our spiritual eye if we do not believe the Bible, which is the word of God. It is impossible to walk in the rest and safety of God's word if we do not believe it. The truth of God creates a peace within us that circumstances and turmoil cannot remove. God wants us to rest in His peace and love, which He provides in His word.

Hebrews 4:9-10
There remaineth therefore a rest to the people of God. For he that is entered into his rest, he also hath ceased from his own works, as God did from his.

We are to rest from our own endeavors of analyzing and trying to figure out how we can solve the situation. We need to rely on God's word and believe that He will see to it that His word is magnified in our lives, which will reflect His glory to all. We have natural desires and ambitions which are normal in our natural life; all these must be submitted to God's plan and purpose for our life.

We need to understand all that God has for us is only attained in this life by having a believing heart, not a heart of fear and unbelief. When we enter into the rest of God's word, we will stop wrestling with the circumstances of our lives and trying to manipulate the person, or persons, in which we are dealing with, and just let God work.

Hebrews 4:11
Let us labor therefore to enter into that rest, lest any man fall after the same example of unbelief.

The labor that we must perform is allowing God's word and thoughts to determine our actions and behavior rather than letting our feelings and emotions take us on a wild roller coaster ride of being up today and down tomorrow, incapable of making stable, concrete decisions. It is not an easy thing to get control of our feelings and emotions. Yet, it <u>CAN</u> be done by the grace of God, within us and upon us.

Hebrews 4:1-2
Let us therefore fear, lest, a promise being left us of entering into his rest, any of you should seem to come short of it. For unto us was the gospel preached, as well as unto them: but the word preached did not profit them, not being mixed with faith in them that heard it.

My brothers and sisters, the only fight we have is to keep our thoughts, emotions, and actions in subjection to the faith in our hearts which is produced by the word of God. The more word we know, the more faith we have. Jesus speaks of "great faith," "little faith," and "no faith." Faith is not a hard thing, it's a spiritual thing. To mentally assent to something is "head knowledge," which is not faith. Faith is of the heart; our heart being our spiritual ear. God's word is spiritual, feeding and maturing in our hearts.

1 Timothy 6:12

Fight the good fight of faith, lay hold on eternal life, whereunto thou art also called, and hast professed a good profession before many witnesses.

So, we see that our fight is for our faith, which only comes by the word of God. "The snake that roars" cannot withstand the faith-filled words proceeding from our heart. Satan's whole agenda is wrapped up in keeping you and I from knowing and believing the word of God. When we know and believe God's word, we have the whole arsenal of heaven as our "hit man."

2 Timothy 4:7

I have fought a good fight, I have finished my course, I have kept the faith.

As I have already discussed, faith as being **F**=**F**ather, **A**=**A**lways, **I**=**I**n, **T**=**T**he, **H**=**H**eart ["Father always in the heart"]. He is ever-present with us in our very own heart. "The snake that roars" would have us believe that God is in heaven on his throne, far from us, but that is a lie. God is living within us, in all His power and glory. He is a Spirit, and we are spiritual beings. Faith is the heavenly, spiritual force *within us*, backed by the Holy Ghost, who executes God's will in our life.

Hebrews 13:5

Let your conversation be without covetousness; and be content with such things as ye have: for he hath said, I will never leave thee, nor forsake thee.

God will always honor His word that is in our heart, as we speak boldly with our mouth. The confession with our mouth is connected to what we believe in our hearts. Our confession before heaven and earth is what causes the promise, the word, to be manifested in our life and the life of our loved ones. As we confess with our mouth God's word and thoughts about us, His heavenly messengers [the angels] are listening. When they hear God's word being spoken, they move to make sure that the word will be brought to pass.

Romans 10:8
But what saith it? The word is nigh thee, even in thy mouth, and in thy heart: that is, the word of faith, which we preach.

God never changes. His modus operandi is the same. He plants His word in our heart, we speak that word, and He causes it to be manifested in our life. We must keep our heart full of the word, so when we speak, all that will flow out is God's word and thoughts. Faith in the heart without being spoken has no life. Speaking brings faith to *life*.

Malachi 3:1
Behold, I will send my messenger, and he shall prepare the way before me: and the Lord, whom ye seek, shall suddenly come to his temple, even the messenger of the covenant, whom ye delight in: behold, he shall come, saith the LORD of hosts.

If you have a loved one that belongs to God, yet they allow Satan to deceive them and draw them backward, you can and must use your authority and the word of God to rescue them. You say, "How is this done"? Simply by seeking God, receiving His counsel, and then speaking that forth in prayer before heaven and earth. Remember, God does not change and He is no respecter of persons. He only respects and honors His word coming from a heart full of faith.

Acts 10:34-35
Then Peter opened his mouth, and said, Of a truth I perceive that God is no respecter of persons: But in every nation he that feareth him, and worketh righteousness, is accepted with him.

God wants us to know and believe that His character is not like man, who can and is persuaded by money, gifts, and prestige. God only honors and respects the person who has reverence for Him and His word. God is not concerned with color or ethnic background, but He is concerned with having a humble and believing heart.

2 Peter 2:7
And delivered just Lot, vexed with the filthy conversation of the wicked.

Lot was a righteous man, meaning he was in right-standing before God even though He made some wrong decisions and was surrounded by ungodly people with ungodly lifestyles. Yet, we see that God sent angels to protect and deliver him from God's judgment.

So, today we may have loved ones and friends trapped and deceived into the same kinds of situations. But through our heartfelt prayers based on the word of God, they can be delivered. Faith-filled prayer releases the power of the God of the universe in our behalf.

Hebrews 1:14

Are they not all ministering spirits, sent forth to minister for them who shall be heirs of salvation?

Church, that is most assuredly you and me! The angels are to minister God's kingdom and all that it represents in our lives, meaning their job is to see that God's word is manifested in our lives. They are doing battle so that the enemy cannot prevail in our lives and the lives of our loved ones. They only move and do battle as we speak God's word [they harken to the word of the Lord].

Psalm 103:20-21

Bless the LORD, ye his angels, that excel in strength, that do his commandments, <u>hearkening unto the voice of his word</u>. Bless ye the LORD, all ye his hosts; ye ministers of his, that do his pleasure.

God's pleasure is to give us the kingdom. He chose His mighty angels to work in our behalf to see that the kingdom is manifested in our lives. As we speak God's word with a believing heart, the angels go to war to see that no principalities, no powers of darkness, and no demons can stop the kingdom of God from coming forth in our lives.

Psalm 35:27

Let them shout for joy, and be glad, that favour my righteous cause: yea, let them say continually, Let the LORD be magnified, which <u>hath pleasure in the prosperity of his servant</u>.

We are God's sons and daughters, His family. He takes pleasure in us having a blessed life. "The snake that roars" would like you to believe something different, but as we have seen, that causes us to have an evil heart of unbelief, which puts us in the enemy's playground.

There is another area of our life that we must deal with in order to maintain our spiritual walk, and that area is "fear." Fear is a tool of the enemy to stop God's kingdom from being manifested in our daily life. It is an emotion from our soulish realm. There is such a thing referred to as healthy fear. This sense of fear should be directed by your common sense.

Tormenting fear is altogether different. It has a sense of doom and dread, which reveals its source as being from "the snake that roars." This kind of fear produces failure, depression, and anxiety. This is not from God. Fear motivates Satan, but faith motivates God.

1 John 4:18
There is no fear in love; but perfect love casteth out fear: because fear hath torment. He that feareth is not made perfect in love.

Brothers and sisters, that simply means that we do not understand how much God, our Father, really loves us. If we are secure in His love (as we should be), we will not fear. When fear attacks your mind and emotions, know that it is not from the Spirit of God. God is love. Love never fails. The depth of God's love when revealed to us, will cast out any fear and torment that may come against us.

James 4:7
Submit yourselves therefore to God. Resist the devil, and he will flee from you.

Whatever area "the snake that roars" is attacking, God has the answer. Seek His face and counsel. Speak what God reveals to your heart. Whenever God shows up, there is only one response, one declaration from His mouth, that being "fear not." So, when we submit to God, He authorizes the Holy Ghost and all of our warring angels to go to battle on our behalf.

Genesis 15:1
After these things the word of the LORD came unto Abram in a vision, saying, <u>Fear not</u>, Abram: <u>I am thy shield</u>, and thy exceeding great reward.

From the very beginning of our covenant until now, at this present time, our Father always says to our heart, "Fear not." In believing those words, we also receive the Holy Ghost as our shield, and God Himself as our reward. Fear cannot remain in the presence of our Holy God and His word. Fear is the enemy of our spirit; we must not tolerate it for an instant. We must learn to recognize it, and cast it out of our mind immediately.

Exodus 14:13-14
And Moses said unto the people, <u>Fear ye not</u>, stand still, and see the salvation of the LORD, which he will show to you today: for the Egyptians whom ye have seen today, ye shall see them again no more forever. The LORD shall fight for you, and ye shall hold your peace.

The same is true of you and me, His beloved children. He always says, "Fear not, trust Me. Believe my word and I shall do the fighting." When we refuse fear by believing and speaking the word with our mouth, the enemy must retreat. Satan knows that he is a defeated foe. The only weapon he has against us is fear, which is what allows him to work destructively in our lives.

2 Kings 6:16

And he answered, <u>Fear not</u>: for they that be with us are more than they that be with them. And Elisha prayed, and said, LORD, I pray thee, open his eyes, that he may see. And the LORD opened the eyes of the young man; and he saw: and, behold, the mountain was full of horses and chariots of fire round about Elisha.

So many times we try to rationalize why God will, or will not, do what He said He would do. We cannot see the way, or explain how it will be done, so we respond in fear of not believing. If our spiritual eyes were open to the truth, there would be no fear. We need God to shut our natural eyes, and open our spiritual ones. God will show us His truth, His revelation, and His deliverance in our heart if we only seek Him, listen, and believe.

1 Timothy 1:8

For God has not given us the spirit of fear [timidity, cowardice]. But of power, love, and a sound mind [self-discipline].

So, we can easily see that fear will not produce any faith in our life. Fear is the opposite of faith. Faith will produce all things that pertain to life and godliness. As a matter of fact, faith is a spiritual law that always produces spiritual fruit. We must treat fear as we would cancer in our body—it must be eradicated and expelled from our minds.

1 Peter 1:3
Blessed be the God and Father of our Lord Jesus Christ, which according to his abundant mercy hath begotten us again unto a lively hope by the resurrection of Jesus Christ from the dead.

Fear is a snare and a trap of the enemy to rob and alienate you from all that your Father has intended for you to have. We need to learn to quickly recognize fear. "The snake that roars" is like a magician when it comes to cloaking fear and the different avenues that he wants so desperately to put into our life.

Proverbs 29:25
The fear of man bringeth a snare: but whoso putteth his trust in the LORD shall be safe.

Fear is always a snare and a trap from the enemy. We cannot receive God's goodness and power thru fear. Fear allows different laws and consequences to be manifested in our life. Satan is the author and creator of fear. In the Garden of Eden, after Satan's deceitful attack, Adam and Eve's first response was fear. Not only did they fear their circumstances, but they feared the presence of God.

Isaiah 35:4
Say to them that are of a fearful heart, be strong, fear not: behold, your God will come with vengeance, even God with a recompense; <u>he will come and save you.</u>

That is our promise, church. Fear cannot stop us if we will only deny it any access to our life. But, rebuke fear in the name of Jesus. Fear has no power over us. The only fear that has power over us is what we allow "the snake that roars" to whisper in our ears.

Now, we must learn to control what comes out of our mouth. The words that we speak allow either the spirit of fear or the spirit of faith to operate in our life. Our words are so very important as they produce life or death. We must rely on the Holy Spirit to teach us the power of words. A good acronym of the term "word" is: **W=Walking, O=Out, R=Righteousness, D=Daily.** The very intent of God's word is to give us abundant life and to keep us walking in the power of righteousness.

James 3:2-6 NIV

We all stumble in many ways. Anyone who is never at fault in what they say is perfect, able to keep their whole body in check.

When we put bits into the mouths of horses to make them obey us, we can turn the whole animal. Or take ships as an example. Although they are so large and are driven by strong winds, they are steered by a very small rudder wherever the pilot wants to go.

Likewise, the tongue is a small part of the body, but it makes great boasts. Consider what a great forest is set on fire by a small spark. The tongue also is a fire, a world of evil among the parts of the body. It corrupts the whole body, sets the whole course of one's life on fire, and is itself set on fire by hell.

My brothers and sisters, this is the answer we need. Our very own tongue can bless us, or destroy us. We must learn how to surrender it to the Lord in His glory and great mercy. This simply means that any weakness, any struggle, any addition can be harnessed and controlled by the very words we speak. Such a simple truth; yet, "the snake that roars" has a veil over the heart and mind of God's people which hinders them from understanding this truth.

We can easily see, church, that all the strength, power, agility and maneuverability of the horse can be controlled by a small bit in his mouth, and so it is with us. Even the grandeur and prestige of the mightiest of ships can also be dominated by a small helm that directs and sets the course as to where the journey ends. Even so, as the Scripture states, "the tongue is a little member, and boasteth great things..." It is dangerous for us to speak out whatever comes to mind, not taking into consideration the consequences of the words spoken.

The Scripture states, "And the tongue is a fire." Our tongue, if not monitored by the Holy Spirit, will allow all that "the snake that roars" can conjure up from hell, to dominate our life. We must guard what we allow into our hearts and minds.

Proverbs 18:21
Death and life are in the power of the tongue: and they that love it shall eat the fruit thereof.

The verse above, literally means that we will eat our words—good or bad, producing death or life. It is up to us to choose which of these two things we want reproduced in our lives.

Our thoughts and words must become a priority in our life. There is no such thing as empty, unproductive words. The words that we speak will most definitely produce either life of death in our life and in the life of our loved ones. We must ask God, in his great love and mercy, to help us keep a watch over our tongue.

Proverbs 12:18
There is he that speaketh like the piercings of a sword: but the tongue of the wise is health.

The words we speak can produce the same results as if they were a sword. The sword can cut away the good, or it can destroy the evil. Our tongue motivated and controlled by the Holy Spirit will produce life and health in our mortal bodies.

Proverbs 15:4
A wholesome tongue is a tree of life: but perverseness therein is a breach in the spirit.

We will bear the fruit of what we speak. Let us be as the prophets of old and pray: "Lord, put a watch over my mouth." We must understand the blessings or severities of the words that proceed from our mouth. With the words that we speak, we are allowing the law of the spirit of *life*, or the law of the spirit of *death* to operate in our life.

Psalm 141:3
Set a watch, O LORD, before my mouth; keep the door of my lips.

Again, we can see that God's intention and provision of his kingdom is for us to control the words proceeding from our mouth. Our lips open the door to blessings or cursings. We choose blessing or cursing simply by what we speak. God in his great mercy and love towards us will, by his Spirit, teach and train our mouth to speak his words and thoughts.

Psalm 34:13
Keep thy tongue from evil, and thy lips from speaking guile.

We should keep our tongue from speaking evil and our lips from speaking guile, which is "deceit." Anything that we speak about ourselves, our loved ones, or the many different situations that occur in our life that does not line up with the word of God is guile and deceit from the enemy. There is only one way to keep our tongue from speaking evil, that being done by keeping our hearts and minds full of the word of God. God's word is always truth, whether we perceive it, or not.

Psalm 39:1
I said, I will take heed to my ways, that I sin not with my tongue: I will keep my mouth with a bridle, while the wicked is before me.

God declares that we must bridle our tongue. Evil is always looking for an entrance in our lives; our tongue is the door keeper of our hearts and minds. Whether we speak life, or death, is our choice. Death produces darkness, and life produces light. God's word is the only thing that will keep us full of life and light.

Psalm 45:1
…my tongue is the pen of a ready writer.

As the pen in hand writes out the thoughts and opinions of the heart, so the mouth speaks out those thoughts and opinions. We must govern our thoughts, opinions, and beliefs by the word of God. As we speak, we are either allowing life, or death, to flow from our tongue. Our tongue is always ready to speak in any given situation, which most of the time is done too quickly.

Proverbs 15:2
The tongue of the wise useth knowledge aright: but the mouth of fools poureth out foolishness.

Our tongue has to be in subjection to our spirit, which is controlled by the knowledge of God's word and His ways. Our tongue can only speak what it can retrieve from within our heart and mind. Our heart and mind are either full of the world's ways and opinions—which God says is foolishness—or His ways and thoughts, which always equals life and truth.

1 Samuel 2:3
Talk no more so exceeding proudly; let not arrogancy come out of your mouth: for the LORD is a God of knowledge, and by him actions are weighed.

God our Father is going to judge every word that we speak by the knowledge of His word. God considers any words or actions that we do outside of his will to be ignorant. His word and ways cause us to be wise and successful in any endeavor that life brings our way.

Proverbs 15:4
A wholesome tongue is a tree of life: but perverseness therein is a breach [breaking, fracturing] in the spirit.

Church, that simply means any word spoken that is not in agreement with God's word is full of deceit! A tongue full of the word will produce life, but anything else spoken, being fueled by man's knowledge and opinions, will most assuredly cause a breach within your spirit.

Matthew 12:36-37

But I say unto you, That every idle word that men shall speak, they shall give account thereof in the Day of Judgment. For by thy words thou shalt be justified, and by thy words thou shalt be condemned.

Jesus, our wonderful Savior and Lord, declared we will be judged by what we speak. Words are so very, very important. They determine the course of our life. They determine whether we are to be controlled by God's plan and purpose, or the plan and purpose of the "snake that roars." words are not to be taken lightly. God's spoken words created the universe; they also create the atmosphere of our life.

Matthew 15:10-11

And he called the multitude, and said unto them, Hear, and understand: Not that which goeth into the mouth defileth a man; but that which cometh out of the mouth, this defileth a man.

Many years ago, the Lord gave me a night vision. In the vision, my mouth was full of worms. He wanted me to understand my words were destroying my life. I was allowing "the snake that roars" to dictate my words which, at that time, were not in agreement with His word. Worms always refer to something dead or decaying. God's word is full of life, and always produces life. Death and darkness cannot survive in the presence of the life and light of God's word.

Exodus 16:20
Notwithstanding they hearkened not unto Moses; but some of them left of it until the morning, and it bred <u>worms</u>, and stank: and Moses was wroth with them.

God had told His people to gather manna, which was a type of Christ, the bread from heaven. In like manner, we must believe, receive, and obey God's word in all that we speak. Everything we say outside of God's word will produce death in our life—and worms feed on dead things. We need the bread of life daily as it is our spiritual food. For our spiritual man to be strong and ensure victory daily, which is God's intention, we must choose his presence and His word.

Isaiah 51:8
For the moth shall eat them up like a garment and the worm shall eat them like wool: but my righteousness shall be forever and my salvation from generation to generation.

God forbid that we, as His body, allow our mouth to be full of worms. **What we speak must become a priority in our lives. We must realize the dire consequences of what proceeds from our mouth.** We must surrender to God's love and grace allowing Him to direct our words. He will direct us to speak His wisdom. A good acronym for "wisdom" is: **W**-word, **I**-ingested, **S**-successfully, **D**-directs, **O**-our, **M**-mouth. So truly, God's word will direct our mouth in any given situation.

Proverbs 23:7

For as he thinketh in his heart, so is he: Eat and drink, saith he to thee; but his heart is not with thee.

Church, our thoughts and words determine our life's course—whether it be governed by hell, or by heaven. The answer is in your mouth, so speak wisely. Remember, our hearts and minds can only speak of what it knows. Therefore, we must begin reading God's word so we will get to know it. Then, we must trust and believe the word of God, even if it goes against our religious traditions.

Mark 11:23

For verily I say unto you, That whosoever shall <u>say</u> unto this mountain, Be thou removed, and be thou cast into the sea; and shall not doubt in his heart, but shall believe that those things which he <u>saith</u> shall come to pass; he shall have whatsoever he <u>saith</u>.

We must realize the importance of words. We either release the power of heaven, or the power of hell with our words. Our words produce life and death depending on their source, whether it is faith or fear. We are spiritual people who are governed by spiritual laws. These are determined by the words we speak.

Matthew 18:18

Verily I say unto you, Whatsoever ye shall bind on earth shall be bound in heaven: and whatsoever ye shall loose on earth shall be loosed in heaven.

With our words we either bind or loose "the snake that roars" in our life. We bind and loose the kingdom of heaven in our life. Brothers and sisters, I challenge you to count the times in the New Testament that Jesus said, "I say." With that in mind, you will never forget that what you say is a testimony of what your life is, and what you desire it to be.

We started this journey at the beginning with words being spoken, then we proceeded to being established with words being spoken, and now we are at our destination which will produce the destiny (a predetermined course of events) that God provided by His word and His Spirit.

So, now we can give Him all the glory, honor, and great majesty that is due Him. He has provided all that we need for this journey. All that we must do is trust and obey— truly, there is no other way. But, Oh, what a glorious, peaceful and joy-filled life!

One last thing I would like to relate that truly sums up all that we have learned and sealed within our hearts. Several years ago, a singing group called "Mercy Me" had a song on the radio called **"Word of God Speak."** That song should be our spiritual alma mater. My prayer for myself and the Body of Christ is, *"Oh my Father, be so merciful and gracious to us, that our hearts and ears would be in awe of Your word and presence ever listening to hear. In Jesus name, amen."*

✦

About The Author

Linda Eddy makes her home in Huntington, West Virginia. She is a born-again Christian who is also a minister of the Gospel of Jesus Christ. She is a member **Christ Temple Church,** whose pastor is Chuck Lawrence, which is also located in Huntington, WV.

Linda is a graduate of **RHEMA Bible Training College**, which is located in Tulsa, Oklahoma, and was founded by Kenneth E. Hagin. She is also a graduate of **Life Christian University**, based in Lutz, Florida.

Linda Eddy is the founder of **Grace word Ministries** which is a Christian ministry whose main objective is to teach the empowering truths of God's word as found in the Holy Bible. Linda enjoys teaching the truths of the Scriptures, especially as they relate to faith, grace, and righteousness.

She also feels it is very important to relate the fact that even though we live in fleshly bodies, we are not to be controlled by our flesh and five senses, but rather, we are also spiritual beings who should be ruled by God's word.

She intermittently serves in the capacity of teacher for selected classes at her home church (*Christ Temple Church*, Huntington, WV).

She also has a heart to teach at other churches and Christian events when invited to do so. If you would like to have Minister Linda Eddy speak at your church or church event, please contact her through her ministry, *Grace word Ministries*. Below is listed her contact information:

Website: www.gracewordministries.org

E-mail address: gracewordministries@yahoo.com

A Note From the Publisher

This book was published by *Kidron Valley Publishing and Promotions (KVPP)*. If you have a book idea which you would like to author, please feel free to contact us, and we will gladly discuss it with you. We offer free consultation in helping you determine if publishing your book with our company is for you.

KVPP specializes in publishing and promoting books by Christian authors with wholesome themes, such as Christian writings, children's books, autobiographies, wholesome novels, etc.

Our book publishing motto is derived from a statement found in the New Testament book of Philippians.

Philippians 4:8
Finally, brothers and sisters, whatever is true, whatever is noble, whatever is right, whatever is pure, whatever is lovely, whatever is admirable—if anything is excellent or praiseworthy—think about such things.

KVPP can publish books in large numbers, but we also endeavor to make book publishing available for those who only want relatively small numbers of books printed, or those with smaller budgets.

We can also prepare e-Books for electronic book-reader devices (such as Kindle) and can list books on venues such as Amazon.com (one of the largest book sellers in the world).

You can contact us through our website—just click the *"Contact Us"* tab. In one or two paragraphs, tell us a little about your book, what you are looking for in regards to publishing, and leave your personal contact information so we can contact you (phone or mailing address). Our website address is: www.kidronvalleypublishing.com